JASSIM
THE LEADER
FOUNDER OF QATAR

To Sir Simon Mayall
with my best wishes

20·02·2022

JASSIM THE LEADER
FOUNDER OF QATAR

Mohamed A. J. Althani

P
PROFILE BOOKS

First published in Great Britain in 2012 by
PROFILE BOOKS LTD
3A Exmouth House
Pine Street
London ECIR OJH

www.profilebooks.com

5 7 9 10 8 6 4

A CIP catalogue record for this book is available from the British Library.

ISBN 978 1 78125 070 9
eISBN 978 1 84765 912 5

Typeset in Bembo by MacGuru Ltd
info@macguru.org.uk

Printed and bound in Britain by Clays, Bungay, Suffolk

FSC
www.fsc.org
MIX
Paper from
responsible sources
FSC® C018072

The paper this book is printed on
is certified by the © 1996 Forest
Stewardship Council A.C. (FSC).
It is ancient-forest friendly. The
printer holds FSC chain of custody
SGS-COC-2061

This book is dedicated to my father,
who first told me the story of Jassim's legacy,
and to my loving wife Hanadi and our children,
Layan, Jassim and Jude

CONTENTS

ILLUSTRATIONS

Map of the Gulf region and Arabian peninsula by Angelo de Conte Freducci, 1555 (© National Maritime Museum, Greenwich, London)

Map of the Gulf region and Arabian peninsula by Rigobert Bonne, c.1760 (© Classic Image/Alamy)

Pearl fishing in the Arabian Gulf, c.1870. (Mary Evans Picture Library)

Bedouin tribesmen in Qatar, January 1904. (bpk/ Ethnologisches Museum, SMB/Hermann Burchardt)

HMS *Philomel* at anchor in the Gulf, c.1900 (British Empire and Commonwealth Museum/akg-images/ Universal Images Group)

Fishing boat and the Diwan al Amiri on Doha seafront, 1950s. (© TopFoto)

Fishermen on the seashore at Al Khor, 1970s. (© TopFoto)

Traditional pearling vessel in 1985. (John Lockerbie)

Bedouin camelriders in the Qatari desert, 1970s. (John Lockerbie)

Bedouin tribesmen of the 1950s. (© TopFoto)

A meeting of tribal leaders in the late 1970s. (John Lockerbie)

Coastline near Fuwairit, 1970s. (John Lockerbie)

The fort at Wajba, *c.*1930. (© Bertram Thomas/Royal
   Geographical Society, London)
The village of Lusail. (courtesy of the author)
Wakra in the 1980s. (John Lockerbie)
Mosque in Doha, 1950s. (© TopFoto)
Sand dunes west of Wukair, 1970s. (John Lockerbie)
Present-day Doha: the corniche. (courtesy of the author)
The corniche at Doha at night. (courtesy of the author)
The modern port of Ras Laffan. (courtesy of the author)
The Pearl Monument, Doha. (© Eric Nathan/arabianEye/
   Corbis)

PREFACE

L ODGED BETWEEN a page-nine advertisement for dentures and the ramblings of a retired Victorian bantamweight, Britain's *Daily Express* published news of a historic visit on 24 January 1935. But in true journalistic fashion, and not stopping to let the facts get in the way of a good story, Lord Beaverbrook's paper made short work of misreporting the first ever official visit by a Qatari emir.

Few Britons had heard of Qatar. And, quite frankly, any Qatari national would have been hard pressed to believe that the headline 'Pearl King with 84 Wives' had anything to do with their head of state's attendance at King George V's silver jubilee. Nevertheless, the article is historic; it acknowledged the Emirate as an independent, sovereign nation-state.

No doubt this fact was lost on readers, whose eyebrows were probably well up their foreheads on learning that Emir Abdullah, son of Jassim bin Muhammad Bin Thani, kept a court of 'astrologers, jesters, dancing girls and dervishes alleged to be gifted with prophecy'. I'm not sure who exactly would have alleged that – probably the editor or some underpaid *Express* hack – and there is no byline on the story either. But whoever wrote the article cannot ever have wondered what it takes to forge a divided, desert peninsula into a nation-state.

To appreciate what it took to create Qatar, we're going to have to use a fair bit of imagination. It's easy to conceive of a time when there were no skyscrapers or schools, hospitals or roads, electricity or air-conditioning. But that is not nearly enough. To credit the true greatness of Sheikh Jassim bin Muhammad Bin Thani's achievements, we'll also have to imagine a land without security or borders, where British sailors and Ottoman soldiers, or Bahraini and Bedouin tribesmen, could – and often did – destroy entire villages.

In short, we'll have to imagine a place where there was no concept of unity except as an idea in one young man's head. Unlike with Kuwait or Oman at the beginning of the nineteenth century, there was no inevitability that Qatar would emerge as a nation in its own right. That it did so, and would become one of the richest and most influential for its modest size, is testament to a truly remarkable man.

QATAR DESCRIBED

Geology, cartography and a little local knowledge

The peninsula of Qatar covers an area of some ten thousand square kilometres, protruding, appendix-like, out of Arabia and into the Gulf. Technically, its surface consists of lower Eocene limestone and gypsum overlain in the south and south-west by Miocene marls and limestone. But to the layman, it is simple low-lying desert with two main folds in the west. This is the Dukhan ridge, where the first oil wells were drilled. These simple hills rise from the coast to a height of just over sixty metres, but extend for over fifty kilometres along the coast and five kilometres inland.

In the centre of Qatar is a gradual swell, known as the mid-peninsula rise, occasionally exposing a limestone of slightly different character from that elsewhere. Indeed, on the southern end and the eastern flank of the Dukhan ridge, the sharply defined mesas and wind-eroded hills make up a very alien landscape. It is this same wind – the north-westerly *shimal* – that blows sand over much of the south-east, where the largest dunes are to be found.

Although the peninsula is contiguous with the Hasa Province of Saudi Arabia, it is separated by vast salt flats.

Travelling here can be a risky business, and the terrain appears to support local tradition that Qatar was formerly an island. This might in turn explain why, until about three hundred years ago, Qatar was often shown on maps as completely cut off from the mainland. But the most intriguing geographical features in Qatar are not to be found near the salt flats or the beautiful inland sea. Rather, it is the subterranean caverns – the *dahl* – which are the most magical. These collapsed caverns contain pools of refreshing water.

Local language

While many of the words traditionally used to describe Qatar's geographic features are known to classical Arabic, most have taken on a more localised meaning. I mention some of these words in part to give the reader a taste for the local vernacular – Jassim's language. This is also a record, however, of a vocabulary that may not survive many more decades in the inevitable march towards development and modernity.

Central Qatar is a limestone plateau, known as the *barr Gatar* – *barr* meaning a stony desert. In Jassim's time, a high rocky hill was known as a *yihzila*, whereas a small low mound was a *hdiba*. The western hills were known as the Mashabiyya. The wind-eroded hills of the east were sometimes known as *gehaab*, and the hills that form a very marked scarp, capped by a harder limestone, were known as *birag* because of the brightness of the rock, which makes them stand out clearly.

The term *nakhsh* means nose and is used for a prominent spur, as in, for example, the plunging end of the Dukhan ridge in the south. Two other terms, *jurn* and *tiwaar*, were also in general use. The former is an isolated horn-shaped hill, whereas the *tiwaar* is a flat-topped mesa.

As elsewhere in the Gulf, place names often begin with Umm or Abu – that is, the mother or father of some natural feature, animal or tribal incident. Some of these places might also have been described as a *rawda* – a semi-permanent grazing area with a well and a very low-lying grass called *naiim* covering it. Less useful pasturage, but with a little water, would be called a *jiri*. Leading into these depressions are small, shallow valleys – the wadis well known in the West. Small, short stream courses in which a little vegetation was to be found were called *shi'b*. A little to the east of the central plateau are the smooth plains, the *rigga*, with a surface of finer stones called *hashu* and a reddish dust, *niiga*.

As the dust-bearing north-west wind, the *shimal*, blows across the peninsula it begins to deposit sand leeward of anything in its path, even tufts of grass. This could be the birth of a dune. This initial deposit is called a *ramla*, or in some parts of Qatar a *bratha*. The *ramla* develops into a long, narrow dune, called an *'irg* by the Al Murra tribesmen, and a *sahib* by the 'Awamir. Both tribes, however, referred to the long, low-lying dune as an *'urgiib*.

Gradually, this small mound would grow into a medium-size dune known as a *zubar*. If it continued to expand, sand would eventually form the individual crescent shape known to geographers as a *barkhan*. These dunes always have their apex pointing towards the north-west. At this point in its development, the dune will grow two arms parallel to the direction of the wind. The gentler-sloping, hard-packed windward side is known as *dhahr al-khait* and the steep leeward side as *sayyal*. Towards the sea these dunes become interlinked to form a sand sea, a *nigyan*. Although there were many different words used to describe dunes, if detail was unnecessary a Bedouin couldn't go far wrong using the word *nagd* – a plain, bog-standard dune with nothing special about it whatsoever!

Water in the area is rare, and a well in the southern desert is called an *'ugla*. There are two popular theories as to the origin of this term. Some say it is due to the fact that the wells are shallow with a depth not exceeding the length of an *'aqal* – the band of cord that kept the Bedouin's headdress on. Others say it refers to the place where a tribe stops and 'ties up'. Whatever the origin, a well wouldn't always contain water. A temporary rock pool on a hill would be called a *mishaash*. But rainfall would gather in geological depressions known as *wa'ab* for longer periods in the winter in the north of the peninsula.

The vocabulary used to describe Qatar's natural features on its coast has ended up in the names of its greatest towns today. A cape is called *ras*, a bay *doha* and a narrow inlet *khor*. The whole peninsula enjoys a small tidal range, small enough for ships to be safely hauled up, repaired and relaunched with a minimum of difficulty. And since the land is low lying, salt pans – the *sbakha* – were created with considerable ease. Low beaches were also encountered inland from the present shoreline and concentrated deposits of shells, called *sabban*, are still found in places that seem very far from the sea.

Maps

Although the peninsula is such a marked cartographical feature, it is remarkable how little information existed about it until relatively recent times. It is not until well into the nineteenth century that the Emirate's outline becomes recognisable on detailed maps. Earlier representations usually showed two large islands, with a varying number of smaller ones, corresponding to Bahrain, and only a slight bulge from the mainland opposite. A river and the 'village' of al-Hasa ran into the sea in the vicinity of the Bay of Salwa. Early references to Qatar are few and rarely extend to more than the name itself. The earliest Arab geographer to mention the peninsula is Ibn Khuradadhbeh in the ninth century, recording it as one of the stops en route from Basra to Oman. Al-Hamdani also mentions Qatar in the tenth century, but only among a list of places in a general description of the Arabian peninsula. It seems that at this time Qatar was seen as a point on a route and not a destination. But even as late as Yaqut and Ibn Manzur of the thirteenth century, Qatar is only briefly noted as a village or town.

The name Qatar would come to be recorded in the West by a man whose entire life was an adventure. The sixteenth-century Portuguese adventurer Pedro Teixeira, who had travelled up the Amazon by canoe, to the amazement of the Spanish garrison at Quito, was also the first Westerner known to have used the name. 'The fishery of Barhen begins in some years in June, but more usually in July, and goes on during that month and August,' he wrote. 'A fleet is formed of about two hundred "terradas" and … commonly goes to fish at Katar, a port of Arabia, ten leagues south of the Isle of Barhen.'

A hundred years later, and following the settlement of the Kuwaiti Al Khalifa at the north-west town of Zubara, historical and geographical details become more readily available. The north-west and east coasts down to the present-day oil terminal of Umm Said, as well as Qatar's pearl banks, were well known and clearly marked by Arab navigators. And following the Persian attack on Basra in 1776, many of the city's merchants took refuge in Zubara, and for a short while the town enjoyed great prosperity.

Even more Qatari names are recognisable on maps of the late eighteenth and early nineteenth centuries, thanks, in part, to the son of a farmer from Lüdingworth, in what is today Lower Saxony. Karsten Niebuhr not only adopted local dress in his travels through Yemen and the Arabian peninsula, but managed to build on his smattering of Arabic to become the foremost cartographer of the Middle East. His 1794 map includes a 'Deh Rogn', 'deh' meaning a village and 'Rogn' referring to Rakan at the northern tip of the peninsula – a prominent landmark for sailors. His earlier map of 1765 also shows Huali and Faraha (al-Huwaila and al-Fareha). On the mainland is 'Khau', which might possibly be Khor Hasan, as well as the Bay of Salwa. And on the map of the Gulf published in his *Voyage en Arabie*, Niebuhr marks the land east of this estuary 'Gattar'.

A more detailed Qatar is well shown on a map in an atlas published by Philippe Vandermaelen in 1827. This Flemish cartographer's *Universal Atlas* had made him very famous in his own lifetime, and spurred various military colleges to invest time and effort in Europe's continuing expansion. His atlas marks four places in a group on the mainland, two of which are definitely recognisable as Core Hessan (Khor Hasan, today known as al-Khuwair) and Jumale (al-Jumail).

By this time, however, a definitive work was well under way. In 1822, after more peaceful conditions had been imposed along the Trucial coast, a British survey of this area was undertaken by the Indian navy, and by April 1825 the two survey vessels – *Discovery* and *Psyche* – had completed their work. One of the officers involved also recorded another first – the earliest documented visit by an Englishman to Qatar. A spectacularly unimpressed Lieutenant Grubb landed at Bida in 1822, clearly missing the gardens of England: 'A most miserable place, not a blade of grass nor any kind of vegetation near it.' It seems, however, that this survey's detailed and accurate naval charts were made readily available neither to the general public nor to the military. Even as late as 1923, the British army's Captain R. E. Cheesman, a keen amateur ornithologist, had to make do on his birdwatching expedition with a map that represented the entire west coast of Qatar as a dotted line!

Nevertheless, the world had become much smaller and the competition between various empires for control in the Gulf would lead to garrisons and explorers opening up Qatar. The German traveller Hermann Burchardt, who traversed the Emirate from Salwa to Doha via Mukenis in January 1904, took the first-ever photographs of the peninsula. A few years later, a remarkably accurate description of the geography of the peninsula and its tribes appears in John Lorimer's monumental work, *Gazetteer of the Persian Gulf*. The British administrator's work can be said to have truly introduced the Emirate to the world.

These days Qatar is a country of gas, oil and opportunity; its rapidly expanding capital of Doha is an extraordinary mix of ethnicities. The native population has increased tenfold since the discovery of oil in 1940. And thanks to its proven reserves of fossil fuels, Qatar now has the world's highest GDP per capita. But today's success was entirely dependent on a generation of men who forged a unified state out of tribal disunity, and a leader who could steer the country clear of foreign and imperial machinations.

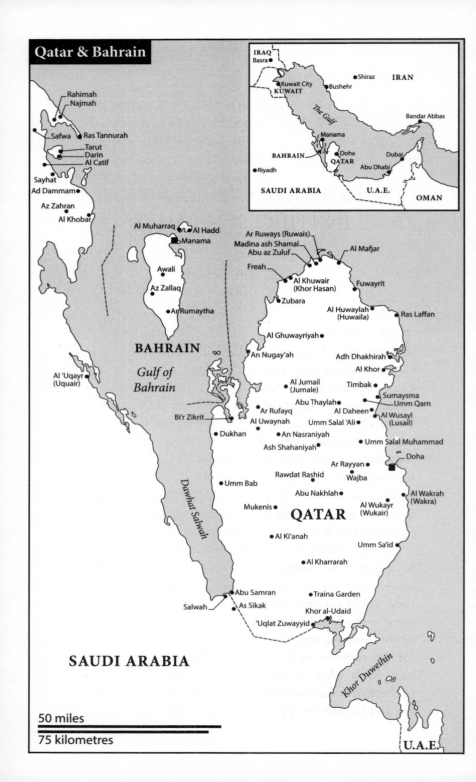

1
_____

INTRODUCTION: 5,000 YEARS
IN THIRTEEN PAGES

I'M GUESSING the ancient Babylonian priest and
astronomer Berosus could tell a story or two. Scepti-
cal readers may not credit his account of how a merman,
Oannes, swam up the Arabian Gulf to gift its peoples with
science and civilisation, but maybe they should. For though
Berosus was no slave to accuracy, he demonstrated a gift
for the symbolic. Qatar owes a lot to the sea, historically
for what was in it, and today for what is under it. And this
sea hasn't given up its treasures easily. For over five thousand years, its waters have ensured that the men living off
it possess great strength of character and mind – qualities
Sheikh Jassim had in abundance.

Oannes wasn't the first special visitor in a region known
to antiquity as Dilmun – the Land of the Living. Should
readers ever feel the urge to read Sumerian sacred poetry,
they would see that there was an altogether more famous
guest – the legendary King of Uruk, hero of the world's
oldest surviving epic poem, *Gilgamesh*. Popping in to search
for the survivor of the Universal Deluge, Gilgamesh was
only doing what any self-respecting civilised human being
in the fourth millennium BC would do. He was looking for
the god Ea, and what better place than Dilmun – a possible

location of the Garden of Eden and Land of Paradise.

Of course, Dilmun in those days covered most of eastern Arabia – but Qatar and Bahrain have always been at its heart. It was by all accounts a fertile, arable land, rather than the present-day desert of undulating limestone. At that time it enjoyed a strategic location between the great civilisation of Sumer to the north and the Indus Valley to the east. It was only a couple of days' sailing south to Magan – today's Oman – and this easily afforded merchants the opportunity to travel between the Indian subcontinent and Mesopotamia. Naturally these merchants would also have traded in the two commodities on offer in Qatar – the beautiful, luminous pearls of the Gulf (referred to as 'fish-eyes') and the dates of the palm trees that sprang up just about everywhere at the time. A growing body of evidence suggests, moreover, that these merchants were none other than the original Phoenicians, who dominated trade along the Persian, Arab and Egyptian shores before moving into the Mediterranean. This may explain why, unlike in other Gulf territories, there is no history of any permanent inland settlement. Archaeological evidence suggests that Qatari towns and villages were only ever built on the coast.

Rivalries

Perhaps the Phoenician exodus in the sixth century BC was due in part to one of the most enduring rivalries of all time. Cyrus the Great of Persia dominated present-day Iran and Turkey, and a sizeable portion of modern-day Syria, Iraq, Lebanon and Palestine for good measure. Nevertheless, despite Qatar's uncomfortable proximity to Persepolis and Babylon, it successfully steered clear of Persian power, though not, it must be noted, of Persian women. Over the centuries, there has been a considerable intermingling of the two peoples. The boundaries of their relative spheres of influence have been complicated by both Arab and

Persian travelling to opposite sides of the Gulf. Both peoples have taken it in turns to escape political or commercial exploitation right up until the beginning of the twentieth century.

But if Cyrus wasn't interested in invading Qatar, Alexander the Great certainly was, dispatching his top admiral, Androsthenes of Thasos, to survey the entire Gulf. Unfortunately for Alexander, this scientist and cartographer was also a great fan of nature and would often feel the urge to divert his trireme, as he pottered round the Gulf, to investigate interesting flora and fauna. What Alexander would have had to say about this, we will never know, as the requested charts arrived shortly after Alexander was poisoned in June 323 BC.

Not to be outdone by Alexander, Rome's most powerful emperor, Augustus, appointed his own adopted son and heir — Gaius Caesar — to mount an expedition into Arabia while just nineteen years old. Clearly, Gaius was a child prodigy — a senator from the age of fourteen, he was voted Prince of Youth and headed Rome's equestrian order at the same time. Gaius ordered several strategic studies to be prepared for the proposed military expedition but promptly got himself killed while fighting in Armenia.

The Gulf was now on the periphery of a great empire rather than next to the centre of one. In effect, Qatar ceased to have the strategic importance it had enjoyed for three thousand years. What this meant for the people who continued to live there must be imagined, as there is no documentary evidence and the next major period of development wasn't to come for another six hundred years. But this was merely the lull before the storm.

At the beginning of the seventh century, Arabs were suddenly propelled to international prominence — and would soon find themselves fighting in eastern China, western Africa and even in Merovingian France. The Islamic conquests were to have far-reaching consequences for most of the world, and the Gulf was no exception. Ruling Qatar and Bahrain from his fort at Merwab in the Joghbi region, Mundhir bin Sawa al-Tamimi embraced

Islam after meeting with the Prophet Muhammad's emissary, Al Ala'a al-Hadrami, in 628. The Prophet's letter of invitation and his seal can still be viewed to this day at the Bait al-Qur'an Museum in the Bahraini town of Hura. Within a couple of years, over a hundred stone houses were built, and Qatar began to gain a reputation as a centre of excellence for its horse and camel breeding, rather than its pearls.

The establishment of Baghdad as the new capital of the Abbasid Empire was also welcome news for the peninsula. The Gulf once more became an important communications and financial centre – a newly reborn trading post. Paper suddenly became plentiful and cheap, following the Abbasid capture of Chinese paper-makers at the Battle of Talas in present-day Kyrgyzstan. Very soon afterwards there were paper mills in most large towns and cities. No doubt the availability of cheap writing material contributed to the growth of the Abbasid bureaucracy, postal system and lively intellectual life. The court of the Caliph, Harun al-Rashid – probably the richest man in the world at that time – was a luxurious one, and Qatar was superbly positioned to provide it with absolutely anything it wanted – textiles and spices from India, porcelain and drugs from China.

Pearling had certainly evolved over the centuries, but now it benefited from the scientific and technological innovations of the period. Detailed maps of the pearl banks were drawn up by the great scholars of the age, as were remarkably detailed lists of the varieties of pearls available – including their shape, weight and price. Scientist and geographer Abu al-Hasan al-Masudi, instrumental in mapping the pearl banks while writing his 365-chapter epic work *Muruj al-dhahab*, was a product of this renaissance. He wrote volumes on Greek philosophy, Persian literature, Indian mathematics and the heritage of the Gulf's ancient cultures. This was also the age of the Sindbad stories, which, while fanciful, pay tribute to the international nature of society at a time when most of western Europe was yet to emerge from its 'Dark Age'. In

short, this was an era when the Gulf was home to a natural association of scholarly-minded people in a highly civilised atmosphere.

Rebellion

Sohar in Oman and Iraq's Basra were the trading ports of the
age. But as their wealth and power grew, so did the social and
political problems involved in their control. Labour shortages in
the sugar-cane plantations of western Iran and the salt mines of
southern Iraq required significant numbers of slaves from East
Africa. At the same time, the minority Shia sect, which had been
kept under strict control, began to take root among the poor.
Slavery and Shiism combined in the person of Ali ibn Muhammad, who, initially basing himself in Bahrain and the Qatari peninsula in the early 860s, proceeded to seek out the blacks of the
Basra plantations to enquire about their living conditions. More
of a young Malcolm X than a Martin Luther King, Ali soon came
to lead what al-Masudi referred to as one of the 'most vicious and
brutal uprisings' of the ninth century. Deaths are recorded in the
thousands. Baghdad was no less vicious in attempting to crush
the slave revolt. When one of Ali's captains from Bahrain was captured and sent with his men to Samarra, the Caliph, al-Mu'tamid,
personally watched as the unfortunate man, named Yusuf, was
flogged two hundred times, had his arms and legs cut off, suffered
extensive burns and then, mercifully, had his throat slit.

Rebellion at the heart of the Abbasid Empire and its Gulf
dependencies didn't end once the so-called Slave (or Zanj) Rebellion was finally crushed in 881. Worse was to come at the hands
of the most lethal vegetarians known to history. The Qarmatians,
who were referred to as 'greengrocers' rather than 'butchers' by
their detractors at the time, were another Shia sect that sought to
establish a utopian paradise at al-Hasa, right on Qatar's doorstep.
Famed for managing to steal the Black Stone from Mecca (it
was returned only twenty-two years later after a huge ransom

was paid) and desecrating its famous well, Zamzam, the Qarmatians persisted in embarrassing the Abbasids for a whole century. They attracted many followers through their messianic teachings. In 906, Qarmatians ambushed and massacred 20,000 pilgrims on their way to haj. Under the Persian Abu Tahir al-Janabi, they came close to raiding Baghdad in 927 and sacked Mecca and Medina in 930. As they collected tribute from just about everyone in the region, and dominated the Omani coast, trade on the Arab side of the Gulf slumped. The golden age was over. From the early eleventh century, any lucrative import–export activity was more likely than not to be found on the Persian side of the Gulf.

The Gulf's sailors still ventured to India and China, but now they were likely to first make port at the newly emerging trading posts of Siraf, on the Iranian coast opposite Qatar, or the island of Kishm, some sixty kilometres farther east. But the safety provided by the Gulf's northern coastline did not extend to Baghdad – which was all but razed to the ground on 10 February 1258. It is difficult to put into words the sheer extent of the destruction wrought by Genghis Khan's grandson on the city – but it was a body blow from which a unified Muslim nation never recovered.

By 1300, Hormuz Island afforded the best protection for trading ships attempting to escape Mongol harassment. At that time, the island's population was predominantly Arab, as were its rulers. The island had salvaged some naval prestige by the fourteenth century, possessing as it did some five hundred fighting ships. Hormuz's authority extended to Qatar, whose pearls continued to provide one of the kingdom's main sources of income. The island was certainly important enough for the Imperial Chinese fleet, under the Muslim admiral Zheng He, to visit in 1414 and again in 1421. But just as Imperial China was winding up naval operations in the mid-fifteenth century, a newly emerging empire had decided to do the exact opposite. The Gulf would never be the same again.

The ship *São Gabriel* rendered the world just that little bit smaller in 1498. Her captain, Vasco da Gama, lost two-thirds of his crew but proved to authorities in Lisbon that circumnavigation of the Cape of Good Hope was possible. Warships sailed, and within sixteen years a fleet under Albuquerque successfully took control of the Arab kingdom of Hormuz by means of a vicious ruse. Inviting the island's young monarch and chief minister to a parley, Albuquerque concluded the meeting with his guests' immediate stabbing.

Antonio Correia completed Portugal's violent domination of the Gulf by conquering Bahrain and much of the Qatari coast, even taking Qatif from King Muqrin ibn Zamil. Correia's descendants, the Counts of Lousa, still keep Muqrin's bleeding head on the family coat of arms, as the family say no Bahraini has ever asked them to remove it. The speed and violence of the invasion were matched only by the swiftness with which a centuries-old intercontinental Arab trading system was dismantled. The cargo transportation, port cities, emporia and communication centres were no more. The financial and legal services recognised throughout much of Asia and Africa were also discontinued. But Qatari woes were only just beginning. Portuguese cannon may have cleared the way in the sixteenth century, but the trading systems of Holland, France and Britain were soon to follow in the seventeenth. The Gulf was now inextricably linked with the commercial and political rivalries of the West.

Not that Portugal was to have everything its own way. Within the space of decades, two forces were to threaten Lisbon's authority and ultimately cause its withdrawal. Starting a promising career as a Mameluke mercenary, Salman Rais was the first Ottoman admiral to give the Portuguese a sound thrashing as they attempted to seize the port of Jeddah in 1517. Though his obvious talents were not recognised by Selim I, Suleiman the Magnificent certainly did recognise them, and sent Rais off on an expedition that was to dent Portuguese strength in Hormuz, Goa and Malacca. He also kept the Red Sea free of Lisbon's warships. And where the Ottomans ventured, the Persians were never far behind. Shah Abbas, the great Safavid ruler of Persia, who had the unfortunate habit of blinding or killing the more ambitious of his sons, was determined to dominate the Gulf. His foreign policy was simple: to exploit the divisions and rivalries of western Europe as they vied for power in the East. Moving his capital from Qazvin to Isfahan, Abbas also knew how to pick his allies, and came to an arrangement with a little-known British trading company that had only just arrived in the region. Granted a charter by Elizabeth I on 31 December 1600, the East India Company was happy to make a deal with Abbas. In 1602, the Iranian army pushed the Portuguese out of Bahrain and then, in 1622, with the help of four English ships, captured Hormuz from the Portuguese, establishing a new trading port modestly named Bandar Abbas.

Concerned at English success, the Dutch and French East India companies redoubled their efforts in the region, and the next hundred years witnessed an intense rivalry between the three nations, involving all manner of political and military shenanigans with local potentates. For their part, both Arabs and Persians were gradually readjusting to the new political environment, while learning how to manipulate it. So it was that Arab tribesmen of the Yariba clan, rather than Ottoman or Persian naval forces, effected the permanent removal of Portuguese power from Muscat and the Gulf. Entering the city on a daring night attack, a small force of determined raiders brought about Muscat's capitulation on 23 January 1650. Flushed with success, the Yariba focused their attentions on Persian-ruled Bahrain – which they managed to capture in 1717 and eventually sell back to the Persians a few years later.

Oman's successes around the Qatari coast might have continued had it not been for Nadir Shah, possibly the last of Asia's greatest military conquerors. Seemingly aware of the comparisons, Nadir idolised Genghis Khan and Timur, and towards the end of his life would even make pyramids out of the skulls of his

vanquished enemies. Certainly, his military genius was as remarkable as Napoleon's – and under his leadership, Persian troops
entered present-day Iraq, parts of the Caucasus, Afghanistan, Pakistan and even Delhi. He was quite determined to extend his rule
to both shores of the Gulf, and was quick to build a navy strong
enough to control a rebellious Bahrain and push the Yariba out of
Muscat. Qatar was under a truly ominous Persian shadow. We will
never know, however, what else Nadir might have conquered, for,
on 19 June 1747, one Salah Bey, the captain of his personal guard,
sneaked into the Shah's tent and thrust a sword into his chest as he
slept. True to his great soldiering spirit, and despite a fatal wound,
the Shah managed to rise from his deathbed and kill two of the
assassin's accomplices before his own demise.

Nadir's assassination was also a death blow to Persian suzerainty in the Gulf. Muscat was almost immediately retaken by
Ahmad bin Said Al bu Said, the Governor of Sohar. Though he
was a shrewd military tactician, Ahmad had no need to fight a
major battle for his success, and success it was. He went on to
found the Gulf's oldest surviving royal dynasty and the first Gulf
state that was never again occupied by foreign forces. Commerce
flourished over the next forty years. By the time his descendant,
Said bin Sultan Al bu Said (1797–1856), came to rule, the Omani
navy was the most formidable force on the Indian Ocean. But
while Oman was enjoying its success, two clouds appeared on
the horizon. First, Britain was establishing its total control over
the entire north-eastern coast of India, a situation that would
guarantee London taking an unwelcome interest in the size of
the Omani fleet as it sought to control the region's shipping lanes.
The second was the rise of the so-called Wahhabi movement in
central Arabia. Sheikh Muhammad ibn Abd ul-Wahhab had died
in 1792, but his ideas for an Islamic reformation and the protection afforded him by a certain Muhammad ibn Saud were to
have consequences that are felt to this day. Ibn Saud pledged to
implement Abd ul-Wahhab's teachings and enforce them on his

and neighbouring towns. They spread despite Ottoman attempts to subdue the movement. The House of Saud would spend the next 140 years mounting various military campaigns and religious missions to control Arabia and its outlying regions, finally taking control of the modern-day Kingdom of Saudi Arabia after the First World War.

In the meantime, while Oman's merchant navy enhanced its trade around the Indian Ocean, a more militaristic naval force was planning to control trade within the Gulf itself. By the end of the eighteenth century, the Qasimi tribal confederacy based in Ras al-Khaimah kept a remarkably large fleet, equipped for warfare as well as trade. It was said to have had around nine hundred vessels, many of which were swifter than European ships. Its naval force consisted of eight thousand fighting men. Naturally, Britain and the Netherlands took every opportunity to brand these ships, and the men who sailed in them, as pirates, though whether London or The Hague actually believed the appellation is a different matter. If one man's terrorist is another man's freedom fighter, then surely one Qasimi 'den of thieves' was actually a perfectly legitimate trading post on the island of Kishm (where, incidentally, Arctic explorer William Baffin had died from wounds inflicted by the Portuguese in 1622). Unfortunately, Arab historians have done a very poor job of refuting the unfounded accusations flung at the Qasimi navy, and the few scholars that have tried are hampered by surnames such as al-Qasimi. In any case, the English East India Company had a major trading interest in the nearby port of Bandar Abbas and so stood to lose a fair amount of its customs revenues when competing with Ras al-Khaimah. In order to protect its profits, a British naval expedition launched an unprovoked attack on Kishm. The Qasimi–British War had begun.

Unexpectedly, Sharjah and Ras al-Khaimah enjoyed nearly all of the initial success in the conflict. Indeed Qasimi power grew rather than abated right up until the beginning of the nineteenth century. Soon the Wahhabis, already keen to expand their influence towards the eastern shores of the Arabian peninsula, were planning to share in the success. Proposing an alliance, Wahhabi forces thereby obtained an arrangement with a navy that could provide safe passage for its trading ships and an opportunity to project Muslim strength against British imperial aggression. Unfortunately for Ras al-Khaimah, the Wahhabi alliance led London to determine that a violent solution was needed to resolve its trade war. In 1809, just sixteen years before Sheikh Jassim's birth, the British launched an expeditionary force against Qasimi headquarters. Their timing was impeccable. The Arab fleet was anchored off Ras al-Khaimah, just waiting to be boarded, burnt and sunk – which is what the East India Company warships *Mornington*, *Aurora*, *Ternate*, *Mercury*, *Nautilus*, *Prince of Wales*, *Ariel*, *Fury* and *Stromboli* proceeded to do. And if the Company's ships weren't sufficient for the job, the Royal Navy frigates *Caroline* and *Chiffone* ensured the town's destruction by disembarking a battalion of the 65th Foot, soldiers from the 47th and an assortment of marines, engineers and artillerymen. The unprovoked attack incensed the Qasimi leadership, who immediately attempted to rally the neighbouring sheikhs of Umm al-Qaiwain, Ajman, Abu Dhabi, Dubai and Bahrain to their cause.

But in vain. The Qawasim were soon to discover they were no longer a match for British sea power, especially after Napoleon's failed effort to restore his empire in 1815. By 1820, after yet another devastating siege of Ras al-Khaimah by British forces, the entire Qasimi fleet was destroyed, as were the towns deemed to have aided their cause. Even the mud-brick Doha, which had had nothing whatsoever to do with the conflict, was destroyed by an over-jubilant East India Company ship administering a solid helping of victor's justice.

The Trucial Gulf

With Dutch and French sea power on the wane, Britain had gained undisputed control of the Gulf's entire coastline. Now it would demand that every region sign pacts which obliged towns and villages to abstain from 'piracy' on land and at sea in return for an understanding that London would rein in its territorial and political ambitions. This system of truces was drawn up in 1820 under the title of a General Treaty of Peace and lasted for well over a century. The seven emirates that today form the United Arab Emirates capitulated immediately. Although it delayed signing, Bahrain became part of the Trucial system in 1861, undertaking to abstain from all forms of maritime hostilities. In exchange, Britain promised to protect the island from attack by sea and, more often than not, to take Bahrain's side in any dispute with Qatar. Neither Muhammad bin Thani nor his son Jassim signed any such truce, however, even in the decades that followed. Indeed, no arrangement was made with the UK until 1916. This was to prove a mixed blessing when Qatar pushed for its independence to be recognised internationally. In Jassim's time, however, the only Arab ships that didn't sail the Gulf flying a flag of truce on their masts were Qatari.

Once these truces were signed, the obvious question immediately posed itself. Which sheikh was responsible for which bit of coast? There were no permanent borders, no maps, no written agreements. Division of authority in Arabia had been in a perpetual tide of change for centuries. Clans were continually on the move, emigrating from island to oasis. But Britain's Trucial system assumed there were clearly defined political units, an issue that would start to resolve itself only once international oil companies established themselves from the 1930s onward. Thus, no sooner was the ink dry on the General Treaty of Peace than all manner of territorial disputes popped up. The 1820 treaty might well have protected British vessels from attack, but it said nothing about preventing coastal wars between tribes. Aware of the issue, the British officials based in Bombay assembled the chief men of Abu Dhabi, Dubai, Sharjah and Ajman once again in 1835, and pressed them to agree, for one year, not to undertake any kind of aggression against a neighbour without first referring the issue to the British. How this sat with the tacit agreement not to get involved in local issues was a moot point. The new truce came to be renewed each year, until Bombay drew up a permanent agreement – the Perpetual Maritime Truce – in 1853. From now on, the term 'piracy' was transformed by British Indian officials into 'maritime irregularity'.

2

THE AL THANI ARRIVE

I lifted injustice for no personal gain
but to see the weaker freed again

POETRY RARELY TRANSLATES well from Arabic,
but the above fragment, written by Jassim towards the
end of his life, seems a fitting place to begin. As his thirty-
five-year rule came to an end, the last Ottoman detachment
was marching out of Qatar, never to return. All tribes recognised his authority. The British were preparing a treaty that
acknowledged Qatar's sovereignty, and Bahrain's demand for
tribute and territory had been scornfully dismissed.

It is a tragedy that no photograph or portrait of the Emir
has ever been found, but then it would also be wrong if we
only had an image of Jassim at the end of his long life. The
young British officials who came to visit the Emir in 1905
and 1911 saw only a venerable octogenarian, a man who
lived in a modest, mud-brick house and enjoyed the simple
pleasures of playing with his grandchildren and tending his
gardens. They didn't see him as the young warrior who, at
the age of just twenty-three, had fought a horseback duel
against one the most feared Bedouin warriors of eastern
Arabia. Nor would they have understood the passions and

adventures of his youth, when he had been hunter and horseman, poet and ambassador, statesman, merchant and even political prisoner.

The twists and turns of Qatar's journey to statehood are absorbing, but no more so than the story of the man so intimately connected to it. Jassim was himself on a journey that began with his birth in 1825 and witnessed his maturing from a brave but rash young man into the grand statesmen and strategist that he surely became. As one British diplomat put it after returning from Lusail, Sheikh Jassim was truly 'a patriarch of the ancient time'.

The diplomat in question was Captain Francis Beville Prideaux, who travelled from Bahrain to Qatar specifically to meet Jassim in 1905. His diary account of the journey is intriguing. Arriving at Bida, which has since been swallowed up by the capital, Doha, he found that Jassim's fort was quite empty of soldiers. The sheikh was in fact a dozen miles away, and Prideaux sent one of the fort's caretakers to ask for transport. The next day, camels and donkeys arrived to escort Prideaux and his entourage. On the journey, he noticed the black camel-hair tents of the locals, pitched just yards from the shore, and would no doubt have observed the women washing clothes in the sea and carrying water from the wells, while the men prepared their nets and saw to their boats following a long but poor pearling season.

As Prideaux pushed into the interior, he would have travelled across rocky mounds where no tree could grow and precious little vegetation either. His diary notes suggest that he was beginning to wonder what sort of palace this Emir of Qatar was living in. He was soon to have his answer, once he looked down on the oasis of Sakhama.

> We surmounted a low ridge and came upon a most refreshing
> and unexpected sight – a garden enclosed by a neat and
> low mud wall, a hundred by two hundred yards in area, and
> bordered by a line of tamarisk trees on all sides. Within were
> three masonry Persian wells of the largest size, worked by

donkeys, and irrigating large plots of lucerne grass as well as a number of pomegranate trees and some 300 hundred date palms ... [within] a small double-storied rest-house and a narrow veranda-like mosque.

A dozen tents surrounded the garden, where the sheikh's body-guard stayed, as well as the servants who tended his mares, camels, sheep, goats and chickens.

A second visit by a newly appointed British political agent, David Lorimer, was undertaken in much the same manner six years later. Lorimer's wife Emily, a great scholar and linguist in her own right, described her husband's meeting with a severely short-sighted, 86-year-old Jassim in a letter to her parents in September 1911. She wrote, bemused, that Jassim had offered her husband two sheep, some hens and a goat, which he'd declined owing to the size of his launch. It must have all seemed very quaint. Yet impressions were deceptive. While Jassim played the part of the old, retired leader, there was nothing that happened on the peninsula that he didn't know about or ultimately control. To understand how he had created a unified Qatar, we must go back to the arrival of the Al Thani on the peninsula, examining how they had come to prominence and something of Jassim's childhood.

The Al Thani were a clan of the Ma'adid, itself part of a very large tribal confederation, the Banu Tamim. In a Bedouin society, most history is passed on by word of mouth, rather than by written record, but such is the fame of the Banu Tamim that we have records going back as far as the sixth century. Among its number are such names as Abu Bakr, the closest friend of the Prophet Muhammad and the Muslim nation's first caliph, as well as two of the Arab world's most famous poets, Farazdaq and Jarir.

The Al Thani

Nomadic by nature, the Al Thani were not settled in any one place, but would wander vast distances over the years, with a few sparse records having them turn up here and there. What is known for sure is that in the seventeenth century they lived around Ushayqir, north-east of Riyadh, in the former province of al-Washm in the Najd. At the beginning of the eighteenth, they moved to the oasis of Jabrin, south-east of the Qatari peninsula. No sources are available describing the motives for their migrations, but it is reasonable to assume drought, pasturage and local trouble all played their part. By the time the Al Thani clan arrived in Qatar in the 1740s, the Banu Tamim to which they belonged had already taken control of the Najd as well as parts of Bahrain and the Yamama. The first Al Thani settlement in Qatar was at Sikak in the south, and from there they moved to Ruwais and Zubara in the north-west.

At that time, authority in the peninsula rested in the hands of the Al Musallam of Huwaila, especially in the north-east. The Al Musallam were part of the Banu Khalid, another tribal confederacy who had driven the Ottomans out of eastern Arabia a hundred years earlier. The Al Musallam claimed the right to collect taxes on behalf of the whole Banu Khalid, so we can probably assume that this was a time of tension, disquiet and confrontation. But the trouble was only just beginning. In the second half of the eighteenth century another two major tribal confederations arrived, the Aniza and Banu Hajir. The former, represented by the Al Khalifa, moved into Qatar in 1766. They had migrated from Kuwait to Zubara, but unlike the Al Thani, quickly constructed the fort of Murair, a short distance from Zubara. From their new fort, the Al Khalifa went on to conquer the nearby island of Bahrain in 1783 – where the family remains to this day. At the same time, the tribe maintained its claim to Zubara and the adjacent Hawar islands – an issue that was not to be resolved until Judge Guillaume issued a ruling on behalf of the International

Court of Justice in 2001 granting the Hawar islands to Bahrain, but retaining Zubara as Qatari. Last to enter the volatile mix, towards the end of the eighteenth century, the Al bu Sumayt settled in the Khawr region while maintaining their strong links to the Najd.

The Al Thani, now led by Thani bin Muhammad, along with the other newly arrived tribes, weren't interested in paying any taxes to the Al Musallam, who effectively lost control. Little is known about the manner in which it happened. All we do know for sure is that Thani was born in Zubara, became a prominent pearl trader and eventually moved his family to the east coast and a village called Fuwairit, where his son Muhammad and his grandson Jassim were both raised.

Jassim's childhood

Jassim grew up in a time of great change. The north of the pen-insula, where much of the population was settled, had often fallen under Bahraini influence, if not direct control. The Al Khalifa were fiercely resisted too, however, and had virtually no power in Qatar in the 1820s. As a result of violent conflict, no coastal settlement was guaranteed absolute safety from attack. The minor settlements in the south-east tended to drift under the influence of what had just become Trucial Oman. The barren central and southern parts of Qatar were incorporated into the lands of the mainland camel herders, and every other year might see one clan triumph over another. There was no concept of a Qatari nation or even a regional state-in-waiting.

But Jassim's childhood was different from that of his forebears. Both his grandfather and father had interests in the pearl indus-try, which necessitated protecting and managing seafaring com-munities. These communities, by the very nature of their work, were far more settled and vulnerable. This shift in Al Thani busi-ness away from pastoralism was to change the peninsula's political set-up. It would lead to the eventual emergence of Doha as the new principal settlement under the Al Thani's aegis. There was a clear model for statehood in Bahrain, which was the centre of the Gulf's international pearl market and a frequent port of call for Jassim's father, who often travelled there on business.

Muhammad was a pious man and saw to his son's education. Jassim was taught to read, write, perform arithmetic confidently and memorise large sections from the Quran by heart. There were no educational institutions at the time, but the quality of Jassim's poetry shows his education was anything but basic. Yet boys will be boys, and we can also be sure he spent many happy hours with his friends on the elevated shores of Fuwairit. It may be that some of the marks scratched by children on to the rocks overlooking the sea – and still to be seen to this day – were created by his hand. The children's carvings consist of double rows of holes that were used for the game called *haluwsah*, in which the holes are filled with pebbles. (It is thought that the pebbles represented the number of ships on the horizon.) The young Jassim would probably have played this game in September, when the children were waiting to spot the pearling fleets coming in at the end of the season. An exciting time, as many of the young boys would not have seen their fathers, uncles and brothers for around four months and each child hoped to be the first to mark their return. But the game could be played all year round, and perhaps with a more serious purpose, such as keeping a weather eye out for a second British attack or warning the town of potential pirates and unknown vessels.

With the sun setting, Jassim and his friends would have been called in to eat the staple meal of fish and dates. In times of hardship, they might even have consumed the date stones that were sometimes crushed for food. *Khubz* or bread, hot from the stone ovens that can still be found in some parts of Qatar, would most likely have been his favourite part of the meal. And on the hottest days, Jassim would have been grateful for the well water, even though it could prove a little brackish. If it tasted too bitter, tribesmen had a habit of drinking it directly through a cloth filter, most often the *gutra*, the traditional headscarf. And at night, a dampened *gutra* would have been placed across an open doorway to help induce a cooler feel for the children as they slept through the intense summer heat. Jassim enjoyed good health throughout his long life, and this was just as well as there were only three treatments for any sickness at the time: bleeding, cauterising or herbs.

Occasionally, Jassim would have attended a *razeef*, the tribal get-together. The experience would have been invaluable, affording him a thorough knowledge of tribal customs, including fun aspects such as learning to perform the *archa* – originally a war dance – in which two lines of men would chant at each other in a competitive and challenging fashion. The Al Thani would welcome guests for days and the prestige of the whole family would have been enhanced, news passed, decisions made and great stories told. And there is one such story, which I shall relate now, that must have had a great effect on Jassim. It showed that one man, in the face of great injustice and overwhelming odds, was capable of bringing an enemy to his knees, through sheer determination and strength of character. Today Rahma bin Jabir is dismissed as a pirate, but he was a pirate in much the same way that the legendary Robin Hood was a thief, or William Tell an assassin.

Rahma bin Jabir

In most parts of the Arab world in the late 1820s, the big news was the rise to power of Muhammad Ali, an Albanian officer who led a palace coup to take control of Egypt. He had established a new dynasty and was successfully projecting Egyptian power into what was to become Saudi Arabia. But his was not the story most often told round any Qatari campfire at the time. The name on everyone's lips was Rahma bin Jabir. To appreciate his story, and why he chose to spend his life making every Bahraini life miserable, requires a few historical steps backwards.

Rahma's father, Jabir bin Utub, had led his people successfully in Zubara when the Qatari town had become a favourite transit point for merchants carrying goods from India to Syria and other Ottoman territories. He had realised that by turning the harbour into a free-trade port he would actually increase revenues into the town. But the Al Khalifa refused to share the economic gains with their kinsman Jabir, and actually forced him to leave the town to settle in Ruwais before having him killed. The Al Khalifa then went on to monopolise the pearl banks around the coast of Qatar. The young Rahma was not to forget what had happened to his father, vowing to make them pay for their greed. And even when he put aside his grievances to aid the Al Khalifa in the face of an imminent Persian invasion, Bahrain's ruling family still refused to share any territorial or political gain with the very family that had helped them to succeed. Thus he returned to Qatar, along with the Qatari tribes of Al bu Kuwara, al-Sulaithi and al-Musallam, determined to take back what was his.

Rahma repeatedly hit the Al Khalifa where it hurt – in their merchant fleet. With the moral support of five hundred dependants, the Wahhabi state and even the Omani leadership, Rahma maintained an embargo on Bahrain from his base at Khor Hasan – which was to become a gathering place for all those who had suffered Al Khalifa injustice. Soon he was seizing, sinking or burning Bahraini ships by the dozen. At that time, Khor Hasan was a dilapidated village whose redeeming feature was that it was protected from the sea by two coral reefs. Only a man with local sea knowledge could navigate through it. Rahma was no fool, and kept himself on good terms with the British – who were keen to keep the Gulf free of all warships save their own. Writing one hundred years later, the British diplomat Lorimer conceded: 'The exploits of Rahma, though in some cases piratical, were performed as a rule under pretext of lawful warfare ... his conduct was scrupulously correct.'

The admission showed publicly that the British recognised the justice of his cause, and privately that it was impossible to stop him even if they had wanted to. But no one could catch Rahma, least of all the Bahrainis, and not for want of trying. Britain's Captain Wainwright of HMS *Psyche* told the Admiralty on 30 January 1820 that getting Rahma out of Khor Hasan was 'full of danger, if not impracticable'. And even when he appeared to have gone too far, Rahma always seemed to have an escape route. He made an alliance with the Wahhabi state and based his fleet at Dammam until his host tired of his war on Bahrain and blew up his home, only to see Rahma escape to his ship and seek out new bases and alliances to continue his private war.

Jabir moved his entire clan to Bushire on the northern Gulf coast and made friends with the local governor, Sheikh Muhammad. He even cheekily dropped into the British Political Resident's office to pay his respects, offering to help His Majesty's navy in its war against Ras al-Khaimah. True to his word, he destroyed eight Qawasim ships, seized four as prizes and even assisted in the piloting of the East India Company ship *Vestal* into the harbour of Qatif when it got into trouble.

Having failed at every turn in its bid to have Rahma killed, Bahrain now decided to pay its way out of trouble, offering an annual tribute of four thousand German crowns to him in April 1820. Jabir took the money, but continued to terrify Bahraini sailors for the next six years. In 1826, however, when Jassim was just one year old, Rahma's luck finally ran out. His death was just as dramatic as his life, and the story was recorded for posterity by the British official Samuel Hennell. We'll take it up as Rahma saw grapnel hooks hurled into his ship by the enemy he so despised.

> [Rahma] took his youngest son, a fine boy about eight years
> old, in his arms, and seizing a lighted match, directed his
> attendants to lead him down to the magazine ... his commands
> were instantly obeyed, and in a few seconds the sea was
> covered with the scattered timbers of the exploded vessel and

the miserable remains of Rahma bin Jabir and his devoted followers. The explosion set fire to the enemy's *baghla*, which soon afterwards blew up. ... Thus ended Rahma bin Jabir, for so many years the scourge and terror of this part of the world, and whose death was felt as a blessing in every part of the Gulf. Equally ferocious and determined in all situations, the closing scene of his existence displayed the same stern and indomitable spirit which had characterized him all his life.

Despite Hennell's opinion, Rahma had shown that it was possible for a determined man to inspire devotion in his followers and fight injustice to the extent that even the strongest enemy could be beaten or bypassed. Stories such as these would not have been lost on someone with Jassim's intellect. Everyone was aware of the strength of foreign forces. By the time Jassim was fifteen, Doha had already been razed to the ground twice, and it would be again in the 1860s. I expect these stories did nothing to counter the impatience of youth, either. As a young man, Jassim found it hard to hide his feelings and demonstrate the thoughtful diplomacy of his later years. When his father chose to receive a British soldier-spy as a guest in Doha, Jassim left town to go hunting rather than meet him. And even when the British explorer and author William Gifford Palgrave insisted on travelling to meet Jassim, their instant dislike of each other was obvious. (Though it must be said Palgrave seemed intent on disliking everything he found in Qatar, describing its towns as dingy, its coffee as unpalatable and its children as brats.)

'Jassim is a more dashing character than his father, but equally close-fisted,' he wrote in 1863.

He is even less amiable than his father [who had just put him up for eight days]; narrow-minded and less well informed than the old man, while at the same time he was more pretentious and haughty. He affects the Najdean [tribesman] in dress and manner, but has far more devotion at heart for the diva pecunia than for the precepts of the Quran. His men, like those of

Justice Shallow, had a 'semblable coherence with their master's
spirits', which rendered their society dry and unprofitable.

Adolescence

But Jassim's society was anything but dry. On a lightning tour of
Arabia to garner information for imperial France and Britain, Palgrave had failed to understand what was in front of his very eyes
as he travelled into the desert to meet Jassim. He saw everything,
but observed nothing. The desert has a number of features that
deeply influence those who live in it. To the Western eye it is featureless and harsh, but to Jassim and his people it had an infinite
and various range of elements that must be understood in order to
survive. Consequently, even to this day, Gulf Arabs are extremely
observant both of the physical as well as the psychological environment in which they live, and can tell a lot about each other just
by the clothes that are worn, and how they are worn. This is hard
to explain to a Western audience, but there is a scene in the 1962
epic film *Lawrence of Arabia* when a suntanned Lawrence has been
given Bedouin clothes and is caught admiring his own sartorial
elegance by Auda Abu Tayi and his young, revolver-wielding son.
      'Son, what fashion is this?' Auda asks, pointing at Lawrence.
      'Harif, Father.'
      'And what manner of Harif?'
      'A Beni Wadji Sherif.'
      'And is he Harif?'
      'No, Father. English!'
      Still, we shouldn't judge Palgrave too harshly, as very few
Westerners ever learn such skills. To understand Jassim, however,
we need to appreciate that he keenly pursued such talents. We
know he enjoyed falconry, and would often, in the late evening,
groom and prepare his hawks for the hunting season, accustom-
ing his birds to the company of others. The young prince was also
fond of his saluki hunting dogs, and kept a couple for many years.

The breed has been used for millennia, and dogs were usually trained to retrieve from the age of three months and accustomed to accept a fairly harsh diet, as they were expected to eat anything that came their way.

In October, at the beginning of the hunting season, Jassim could at last spend days on end out in the desert, the approaching winter making the occasion that much more enjoyable. The Saker falcon, or *Falco cherrug*, was the preferred species, rather than the peregrine, as it was considered to have more intelligence and aggression, and a greater tolerance to stress. Jassim would have used the female of the species, which is still the practice to this day. Further training would have been carried out with pigeons, and it was a common sight at that time of the year to see birds flown to keep them fit and effective. The bustard, or *hubara*, was the traditional quarry, as well as the desert hare. Both made for good sport, as the *hubara*, though a slow, large bird, goes to ground readily, making it difficult for the falcon to follow. Sakers were usually taken as young from their nests or trapped abroad as mature birds, but Jassim would still have needed to personally spend time with them, as it is only when trust and understanding have developed that the sport can really take place.

Jassim and his friends would have spent much of their time at the start of the season handling the birds and talking about them with friends. In the evenings, they would have sat near a campfire, the curve-spouted *della al qahwa* (coffee pot) kept warm by the flames. He and his guests would have drunk coffee made from ground green beans, and brewed with cardamom, which was served in small cups – the staple drink in all social settings. The Bedouin tradition has always been one of extreme hospitality, and the Al Thani were no exception. As his humble home at the end of his life suggests, Jassim did not seek out luxury and was happy to live in the manner of the guards who protected him. He would have sat on the ground and shared food from the same dish as his friends and guards.

These desert outings were no self-indulgence but rather an opportunity to learn and develop many skills. Most important of these was knowledge of how to navigate round a featureless desert. There are few places that easily betray their location in Qatar's interior, though in very dry years near Mesaieed there are dunes that are said to 'sing' when the wind blows, a most eerie sound that was usually ascribed to evil jinn spirits. More normally, the sun, the shape of dunes, the breeze and the stars were the tools required to appreciate position. Even to this day, old men will tell anyone willing to listen how it is possible to 'taste' the wind and listen for different types of 'silence'. The thing is that such stories can't be dismissed out of hand, because the simple truth is that these men did get around the desert without a compass or GPS system.

We know Jassim was keen to enhance such skills, and loved keeping the company of men who had performed amazing feats of endurance. He often went hunting with two Bedouins in particular – one from the Menasir clan and one from the Murra – because they had successfully crossed the great Empty Quarter, the Rub' al-Khali, making it to Yemen and back again. There were still people being smuggled from Yemen to Kuwait in the 1950s who didn't survive a similar journey, despite travelling in specially adapted desert vehicles. For these two tribesmen to have survived the return trip as well, without getting killed, lost or dying of thirst, was remarkable. Journeys such as these have brought fame and fortune to many a Western traveller who has published accounts of their privations, and such tribesmen were also honoured in their own societies.

His desert outings would also have afforded Jassim opportunities to hone other skills. He would have learned how to handle a rifle, ride bareback and fight with sword and lance. Arabian horses have been famous for thousands of years, and their bloodline is still used to bring speed, endurance and strong bones to other breeds. With their distinctive head shape and high tail carriage, they are probably the most easily recognisable horse breed in the world. But they are also one of the oldest, and have been bred in Qatar for over four thousand years, exported only in recent decades. Although Westerners tend to think of the Bedouin association with camels, in Qatar it was the horse which the tribesman prized more, especially for its mobility and manoeuvrability in battle. This was in sharp contrast to the heavy European cavalry, as deployed by soldiers such as Prince Rupert of the Rhine. At the Battle of Edgehill, for example, it took his cavalry a whole hour to re-form for a second charge, by which time the fighting was over. Jassim loved his horses fast, strong and intelligent, much as young Qataris love their fast cars today.

Oddly enough, these equestrian skills have remained with the Al Thani to this day. I don't know whether you can imagine riding up a wet, narrow, thirty-degree ramp over a hundred yards high in front of tens of thousands of people, while holding aloft a burning torch. The great-great-great-grandson of Jassim performed such a feat at the opening of the 2006 Asian Games in Doha. In a radio interview the next day, it was noticeable how Muhammad bin Hamad referred to his horse as if it were not only a human being, but a friend and companion, constantly using the word 'we' to describe his and his horse's exploits the day before.

Jassim's respect for the Bedouin lifestyle was also made clear from the clothes he chose to wear. His father, Muhammad, preferred the dress of the seafaring Trucial coast – such as you might see in Oman today. But the son preferred the dress of the Najd Bedouin from a very young age. Jassim was one of them, and was shortly to prove he had acquired their bravery and skills. For in 1849, at the age of 23, Jassim led his tribesmen at the Battle of Mesaimeer against one of the most famed desert warriors of the age – Musa'id. No written account of the battle survives, but we know from oral tradition that Jassim charged directly, brought down Musa'id with his lance and led his men to a successful defence of the town. Jassim's childhood was over.

3

AN INDUSTRY IN NEED OF A GOVERNMENT

The Pearl that the Prince full well might prize
    so surely set in shining gold!
The pearl of Orient with her vies
    to prove her peerless I make bold:
So round, so radiant to mine eyes,
    smooth she seemed, so small to hold
Among all jewels judges wise
    would count her best an hundred fold
Alas! I lost the pearl of old!
    I pine with heart-pain unforgot;
Down through my arbour grass it rolled,
    the pearl, precious, without spot.

THE WONDROUS PEARL has kept poet and painter employed for centuries, as this adaptation of a fourteenth-century Lancastrian poem proves. It has been a metaphor for all that is rare, beautiful and admirable since biblical times, used even to describe the adornments on the gates of paradise and, in the Quran, the clothes of those fortunate enough to be there. The West's fascination for the perfectly spherical little globules of concentrically coated, crystalline calcium carbonate has remained constant over the years. Could Johannes Vermeer have placed anything else at the very centre of his portrait *Girl with a Pearl Earring*? With such a title, presumably not, though Holland's answer to the *Mona Lisa* is admittedly quite pretty too. And what else could Jack Sparrow, fictional captain of the Hollywood film *Pirates of the Caribbean* and its sequels, have named his beloved ship? *The Pearl* certainly trumps *Queen Anne's Revenge* in my book.

Pearls were craved by the West's wealthiest and most attractive women for hundreds of years. The Austrian beauty Marie Antoinette, whose mother's face was stamped on to the Maria Theresa dollars used to pay for many of these pearls, was seldom painted without them. Empress Maria Fiodorovna, mother of the last tsar of Russia and a society-shocking swimmer, was positively dripping with pearls in her 1880s portrait by Ivan Kramskoi. Margharita of Savoy, Queen of Italy and mother of Victor Emmanuel III, had one of the longest pearl necklaces of the twentieth century. She was often photographed proudly wearing it too, despite suffering the dubious honour of having had a pizza named after her in 1889. In short, the clamour for pearls had never been so loud, and it was the Gulf which was required to provide them. For until the settlement of the Americas and the West's domination of trade with China and Japan, there was only one place for Europe to slake its thirst for these exotic jewels – the Arabian Gulf.

Thus it was that towards the end of his life, Jassim ruled over a twenty-thousand-strong nation, half of whom dedicated the best years of their lives to searching out *Pinctada margaritifera* and *Pinctada radiata*. Jassim's father, Muhammad bin Thani, described Qatar's social and economic dependence on the gems best to William Palgrave in 1863: 'We are all from the highest to the lowest slaves of one master … the pearl.' But Palgrave didn't need to be told. The Arabic-speaking spy, who would often pretend to be Muslim, made extensive notes on everything he saw and thought. He observed the dramatic health effects pearl hunting had wrought on Muhammad bin Thani's closest friends and advisers, describing them as 'sallow-faced … their skins soddened by frequent sea-diving and their faces wrinkled'. One thought that didn't occur to him, however, was that these very same jewels would eventually help provide for Qatar's independence.

By the end of the nineteenth century, the demand that drove the expansion of pearling was truly global. The British Empire was a prodigious consumer, as were Europe and the United States. London's political agent in the Gulf observed in 1910 that 'the demand for pearls is more than equal to the supply … and revival in the prosperity of Europe and America is immediately followed by a corresponding rise in the value of pearls'. Another British official noted in 1915, two years after Jassim's death, that should the supply of pearls fail, Kuwait, Bahrain, Qatar and the ports of Trucial Oman 'would practically cease to exist'.

All the more incredible, then, that a trade which had begun some seven millennia earlier, and which employed most of the men and boys on the peninsula, should have suffered such a swift demise. The Great Depression of 1929 choked off any excess wealth that might otherwise have been spent on adorning the necks of the West's wealthiest women. But depressions had come and gone before. In 1907, the market collapsed and Jassim had to sell the nation's pearl harvest at half the price he had paid for it – losing some six million Indian rupees in the process. After sending his son to Bombay to investigate, the sheikh was forced to establish Doha's first customs house. Clearly, then, Qatar's fortunes were tied to the price of the pearl, and fluctuations in the market had dramatic consequences for everyone involved. The Depression was not enough to end pearl hunting, however. The Gulf's main industry was instead eventually brought to its knees by a couple of researchers thousands of miles away in Japan.

Should you really wish to point a finger of blame, then point it at biologist Tokishi Nishikawa and his carpenter friend Tatsuhei Mise, who discovered a technique for inducing the creation of a round pearl within the gonad of an oyster at the beginning of the twentieth century. Entrepreneur Mikimoto Kokichi shortly thereafter patented an industrialised version of the technique, and the first successful harvest was produced in 1916. By 1935 there were three hundred and fifty pearl farms in Japan producing ten million cultured pearls annually. Traditional pearl hunting in the Gulf was all but dead. Qatar's final *boom*, or large seagoing boat, was built in the early 1970s, and all signs of a once proud industry were erased by the year 2000, with the official closure of the Gulf's last pearl-oyster market in Kuwait. Occasionally, you can still read of businessmen in the Gulf who dream of getting their hands on the pearls that have not been harvested in the Gulf for so many years, only to discover that the skills for finding them have gone for ever. The *nakhoda*, or ship's captain, was an expert in finding the pearl banks, guided by the sun, the stars, the colours and depth of the sea. The divers knew to leave younger oysters, and which ones were likely to contain a pearl. These were skills and knowledge gained over centuries, but lost overnight.

Lest one feel the pang of nostalgia too keenly, it should be noted that pearling was a desperately hard life for almost every Qatari involved. The financial and physical strains were harsh and the rewards barely worth the effort. If a market collapse was tough on the ruling Al Thani, you can be sure it was truly dismal farther down the economy. Financial regulation was well defined, and debt was as soul-destroying as any prison sentence. Ship's captains usually borrowed money from a specific kind of businessman, the *musaqqam*, at the beginning of the season. Out of this loan, they would pay for provisions and cash advances to divers, whose wives would have to make do without them for four to five months of every year. If the captain could not in turn repay his debt by season's end in September, he sold his entire crop to the *musaqqam* at around 20 per cent below market price, losing the whole season's profit. To avoid this, captains charged the divers very high commissions for the advance on their pay. Admittedly they allowed for repayment in instalments, but divers owing money to captains often became so mired in debt that they were obliged to work off their loans or pass them down to their sons as an inheritance. In effect, some sailors were born for the privilege of working to pay off a loan they had never taken out.

Ironically, it was often the case that many of the peninsula's black slaves were in a better situation than their 'free' shipmates. Slavery in Qatar wasn't officially banned until 1952, but before gasping too loudly, know that Doha was ahead of the game. Indeed, it abolished the practice before Saudi Arabia, the Trucial States and Yemen. Oman didn't even get round to ending slavery until 1970. But the word slavery should not evoke the cotton plantations of the Deep South, where the foreman's whip was law and the segregation of races sacrosanct. It is true that half of the pearling population of Qatar were slaves or former slaves, but it is equally true that many of them had become part of the families they had originally worked for. Intermarriage was not a taboo and, on these pearling expeditions, slave and freeman ate the same food, slept on the same deck and used the same *zuli* to answer the call of nature. And as with diamond and gold mining today, those Westerners in the market for pearls didn't ask many questions about working conditions at the time.

True, once Britain became actively involved in the Gulf, it made a number of agreements with the rulers of Bahrain, the Trucial States and Muscat that bound them to suppressing and abstaining from the slave trade. Some British naval officers even stopped ships to set blacks free. But in Jassim's time, Qatar had no understanding with Bombay or London and kept its slave work-force at their duties, be they fishing, pearling, guarding or even acting as the scimitar-wielding emiri bodyguard. When Doha finally signed a treaty with imperial Britain in 1916, however, Jassim's son undertook to enforce the same anti-slavery regulations as other Trucial coast rulers. He and his people were allowed to retain slaves already in their possession on the condition, as the British put it, that 'they treated them well'. But Britain was often frustrated to find that the domestic slaves it was now so keen to liberate preferred the economic stability of a guaranteed roof over their heads, especially during the 1930s, when financial hardship was at its highest. Tellingly, the British promised to issue certificates of manumission to any slave who wished to be freed; yet in the 1920s and 1930s the annual number of manumitted slaves rarely exceeded two dozen for the entire Gulf region.

Whether slave or freeman, however, if either could cope with the financial hardship, pearling itself was just as desperate a business. Forty years ago, the Kuwaiti film director Khalid al-Saddiq produced a feature film that resonated with many of his grandparents' generation. *Bas ya Bahar*, which has been roughly translated as 'The Cruel Sea', is set in the 1930s and tells the tragic story of a young man's struggle to earn enough money to marry his childhood sweetheart and pay off his father's debts. Surviving the heat, discomfort, sharks and jellyfish, he at last finds a wondrous pearl that might pay for his modest dreams to come true. But fate decrees he must perish beneath the waves after his hand becomes stuck in an oyster bank. When his grief-stricken mother is given the pearl, she hurls it back into the very sea that has caused her family so much pain.

The conditions under which divers worked were abominable. Men – any male over the age of about twelve – would leave their families for months on end during the height of summer. Boats that were meant to carry six or seven were more likely to carry 26 or 27. Just five years before Jassim's birth, the British made every effort to limit the size of native boats still further, and it was quite common for them to be so overcrowded with equipment, food and water that there was hardly any room for the crew to sit, let alone sleep at night. During the day, the men could expect to work in temperatures of 45 degrees or more. One can only assume that, if there was no breeze, the heat and humidity must have made pearling a living hell.

The days were long and arduous. Divers were in the water

just after dawn and often stayed there until dusk, stopping only to literally catch their breath. A diver's equipment included a string bag in which to gather the oysters, a goat-horn clip for his nose and a rope tied around his waist by which a partner on the boat pulled him up at the end of each dive. A typical swim would last about two minutes – time enough for an experienced man to grab about thirty oysters from the sandbanks some twenty metres below – followed by a rest of only a minute, although most captains would give their pearlers a longer rest after every ten dives.

At times, a strong wind might prevent diving or, occasionally, the crew would have to row their becalmed boats from one location to another. It was exhausting work that would wear down even the toughest. But then they could not afford to slow down, fall ill or ask for rest – not so much in fear of a captain's punishment, but because they might have their share of the season's income reduced. Sailors were paid only when the season was over and the pearls had been sold or traded to the merchants who would export them to India. A tenth of the profit went to the shipowner, 20 per cent for the provisions. The remaining monies were divided between crew and captain – who received three shares to a crew member's one. In later years, Sheikh Jassim would also receive one share from each boat in the fleet for the protection he provided their villages while they were away. Later he would introduce a tax as well. Ultimately, crews would have been able to provide food for their families, but little else.

Working around twelve hours a day in the sea had serious consequences for health, and not just in terms of such obvious dangers as predatory sharks! By the age of about twenty-five, most men would already have begun to suffer painful skin and eye afflictions that could be treated only with herbs. If a diver surfaced too quickly, he risked damaging his ears; too slowly and he might just drown. Diving ended once the light had begun to fade, affording a rare opportunity for these men to eat a proper meal, as diving on a full stomach was impossible. As a result of months of malnourishment, many of the men would lose their teeth. The only types of food to be had would have been dates, salted fish and possibly a little rice. Fresh water was in fact often brackish, and would have had rather a unique taste – being drawn from rusty iron barrels on supply boats that serviced the pearling fleet. After they had caught a few hours' sleep, the real work would begin at first light. The previous day's oysters were waiting to be opened. They would have been piled high on deck and left overnight to weaken or die before being prised open and checked. Although the crew were eager to find pearls, they would also keep back any shells that had particularly beautiful mother-of-pearl. The best nacre came from a third species of oyster native to the Gulf, the *Pteria macroptera*.

Despite their lot, the crew no doubt put a brave face on things, and a whole musical genre evolved over the decades that helped make the best out of it. Sea shanties, or *fijeeri* songs, were common throughout the Arab Gulf. A lead singer, or *nahham*, would be backed by a chorus of accompanying voices. As opposed to the Ladies-of-Spain-type songs of the British navy, these shanties were invariably about Allah, the ship, the wind and the sea. Every job had its accompanying rhythmic motion, and the 'pull and haul' songs of the Gulf are truly beautiful. Author and adventurer Alan Villiers wrote up his impressions in 1939 on seeing one such expedition leave port. (Unknowingly, Villiers was himself about to join Britain's Royal Navy and play a part in Operation Dynamo at Dunkirk.) His description of a Gulf sea shanty is almost as hypnotically captivating as the song itself.

> With sufficient volume of menacing growls, the soloist, striking a higher note, suddenly quickened his pace and all hands fell at once upon the halyards. The deep growling stopped and the sailors took up the song ... the sweat poured from them; the song swelled; the taut yellow-line stood rigid as steel as those great muscled arms brought it down, down. The blocks creaked, protestingly; the loosened parrals groaned; the yard trembled

and quivered along its length. Up, up it went! The blazing sun beat down and there was no shade; the very sea burned with the sun's fierce light, and the sweat ran in streams. This was brutal work. It was difficult to keep foothold as they stamped and stamped again their great, calloused feet on the wooden decks and hauled and sang.

Unfortunately, Villiers didn't get to hear Qatari women singing their cycle of songs, or at least he didn't note it, for wives, sisters, mothers and daughters would also gather on the shores to sing out to sea for the safety of their husbands on their voyages. And what long voyages they were.

In Jassim's time, the season was divided into three parts. The first part was called the *ghaws al-barid*, a forty-day expedition in mid-April. The main event, the *ghaws al-kabir*, commenced in mid to late May and ended some time in September, or even early October. Lastly, for those desperately poor enough to need it, the *rudaida* was an additional possibility. There was a week's leave between the three stages, when the sailors could return to their home ports to rest and reprovision. After October, no ships could be used to hunt pearl, but in the winter men were allowed to wade out on to some of the extensive shallow banks to try their luck. The practice, known as the *mujannah*, was great for the lucky few who found anything because such pearls could be collected tax free.

Once safely home, after five months at sea, it would usually take the men three months to recover from their exertions – not just because of undernourishment, but also the early signs of scurvy and the like. Some of the younger teenagers would also have to cope with complications to their still-developing lungs and respiratory systems. One can only imagine the desperation when the oyster harvest had largely failed – as occasionally happened – and ships had little to show for their efforts. Nevertheless, it is a tribute to these men's strength of mind and body that no one else seemed capable of farming the pearls for themselves, and not for want of trying. The Dutch attempted as early as 1757 to cut out the Gulf Arabs altogether and harvest oysters directly. They didn't even last one season. And even though the British were well acquainted with the more advanced technologies used in the Sea of Japan and the Far East, and stationed steam-powered vessels in the Gulf region from the 1860s, yet still they were of the opinion that the effort and sacrifice needed to obtain the pearl did not justify the reward.

Jassim would have had to protect not only these men's families but also the industry itself. As early as 1790, Qataris were noticing that the oyster banks around the western shores were furnishing declining numbers of pearls, and there was discussion of the environmental impact of the industry on the sea, well before it became the trendy, 'green' topic of recent decades. *Nakhodas*, or ships' captains, were worried an increasing demand for mother-of-pearl meant that fewer shells were being returned to 'fertilise' the bed. Even the British noticed it, with one Hartford Jones reporting that the sea 'has latterly not proved so productive as in former times'. Some *nakhodas* were sent to find new beds, locating *hairaat*, or underwater mounds surrounded by deep water, so as not to over-farm the traditional *najwaat*, or ordinary, eight-fathom-deep banks. But the growing demand meant the market would not be denied, and regular boosts in production saw a 350 per cent increase under Jassim's rule. With declining numbers of quality pearls, demand outstripped supply and prices went through the roof.

Comparing values of money is not straightforward because figures can be calculated in many different ways. Items that might be expensive today (boats and labour, for example) were often comparatively cheap then, and vice versa. So, depending on which economic historian you ask, £500 sterling in 1850 might be just £40,000 in today's money, using retail price indices as the basis for comparison. But if a measure of gross domestic product is used, that same £500 might be worth a cool million. Secondly, of course, the pearl merchant, the *tawwash*, never obtained the true value of the pearl, and, in descending order down to the divers, the proceeds compared to the perfection of the pearls were low. The general point is: figures are guesstimates at best. I'll put £500, then, at £200,000 today and tell you that Qatar's pearling industry in 1850 was probably bringing in about £40 million in today's terms, and three and a half times as much by 1905. Not bad for a country whose total population was less than 22,000. Of this money, the ruling Jassim would have received about 1 per cent. Indeed, the historian Rosemarie Zahlan reports that Jassim collected £750 in 1908, about £350,000 today.

No one in their right mind would have begrudged him the revenue. The task of protecting the coastal settlements from Bedouin raiders was probably one of the easier of his many duties. What made Muhammad and Jassim's lives more difficult was the constant threat of Ottoman domination, and poor relations with British Indian merchants, who, when the opportunity arose, would call on the government in Bombay to regulate the market in Doha, if not actually invade. And then, of course, there was the possibility that a European recession or war might lead to a market collapse, inducing social upheaval or starvation. Worst of all, the British still had a habit of burning significant sections of Qatar's pearling fleet, as last happened in 1896.

More money matters

Anyone visiting Qatar today can't fail to notice the large number of foreign workers from Nepal, India, Pakistan, Iran and the Philippines. But only those of the last ethnicity are in fact recent arrivals. In the nineteenth century, many men from the Indian subcontinent earned their living in the Gulf. Qatar was no different from its neighbours in this respect. Indeed, the Indian rupee was as widely accepted as a Maria Theresa dollar, an Iranian *kran* or a British gold sovereign. The German mark was also accepted later in the 1870s. Qatar didn't print its own currency, the riyal, until 1966. The Maria Theresa thaler was a silver coin that had become stuck in a fiscal time-warp. All coins had to be dated 1780 as far as Arab traders were concerned – even though they were being minted right up until the early twentieth century. And though the coin had started life in 1751 during the reign of Empress Maria Theresa, who ruled Austria, Hungary and Bohemia until 1780, the coin was so popular that the buxom Maria was stamped on to 39 million thalers in the noticeably un-Austrian cities of Birmingham, Bombay, London, Paris and Rome, never once to jingle in a Habsburg pocket. (The *kran* was accepted in Qatar until Persia ceased minting it in 1932. It could be subdivided into *shahis* or *dinars*, and was worth one tenth of a *toman*.)

With a fair few nationalities working in Doha, it is small wonder that problems occasionally reared their ugly head. One such instance was to have serious consequences with the Indian pearl merchants in the early 1880s, and Jassim's relations with these British subjects proved especially problematic once the industry started to bring in serious money from around 1875. The unhappy upshot, as will be explained in detail later, was that by the beginning of the twentieth century, there was only one resident Indian in the whole country. This very fact alone was enough to distinguish Qatar from all other Gulf societies at the time. But India's loss was Persia's gain, and the percentage of Qataris with Iranian origins is significant.

There were other major changes too. Jassim was the first ruler to be able to levy a tax on all pearling ships from around the entire Qatari peninsula, which formed the basis of his revenue. His father had been able to levy tax only on boats from Doha and Wakra. The new emir ended his father's practice of imposing different rates of tax on different tribes. For example, Muhammad had never been able to get a single rupee out of the Al Sudan tribe in Doha. It took Jassim a few years, but we know that by

1908 they were paying the ship captain's tax, at the same flat rate as everyone else. The tariff on every *nakhoda*, hauler and diver was four Maria Theresa dollars, two for each apprentice. And with a genuine state income came genuine state institutions. By the 1890s, Qatar had its first proper roads and ten of the nation's first ever schools were opened.

The pearling season largely determined the fortunes of the state but there were also attempts to diversify and generate greater revenue from other industries. The sea, already giving so much, provided Qatari shipping with a further two money-making enterprises: fishing and transport. Fish of all kinds were plentiful and a staple part of the region's diet; the fishing fleet was around a quarter the size of its pearling one. *Hamour*, or grouper, makes for a popular meal today, but there were literally scores of species to choose from then, including red mullet, sea bass, red snapper, red tuna, red-banded sea bream, mackerel and the small but mouth-wateringly delicious rabbitfish or *Siganidae siganus*, known to locals as *safi*. Catches were sold in Bahrain, and as far north as Iraq.

Similarly, lateen-sailed transport ships, the aforementioned *booms*, carried goods to the ports of Bahrain and Lingeh and their design was modified as ships were once again used for purposes other than pearling. Despite a romantic image, the lateen sail already had a particular advantage over its European rivals before the industrial age. Its fore-and-aft rig could be used to sail closer to the wind than the West's square ones. They used smaller sails than those of the equivalent European craft but, with their long keel, shallower draught and lighter weight, they tended to be faster. This combined with easier manoeuvrability, with craft often sailing around a head-on wind rather than tacking, to say nothing of a sailor's local marine knowledge, giving him significant advantages over rivals.

Still, in Jassim's time, Qatari boat-makers modified their boat designs in the face of European transport competition. Boats had traditionally been made with teak planks connected with coir rope bindings and heavily greased. This had given them literally flexible craft, better suited to dealing with the sandbanks and reefs of the Gulf. But they came to incorporate the nailed oak planks of the British navy, and dhow boat construction developed, using wrought-iron nails driven through bow-drilled holes packed with hemp soaked in an oil and tar mix. The new designs were strong enough to carry heavier cargoes. Regretfully, no dhow or *boom* has been laid down in Qatar since 1970; no shipbuilding of any kind has survived. The few retired Qatari shipwrights who remain describe how natural and organic their constructions had been. Traditionally, for example, the ribs of the ship were left more or less as the imported trunks and branches arrived, trimmed only at their junctions with the planks of the boat.

In the West, where sailors are married to their jobs, ships are all female. But the Gulf's dhows were a more equitable mix of male and female, though I'm not sure feminists would be overly pleased with the result. Ladies had short, fat prows, while the gentlemen enjoyed fine, long ones. Be that as it may, such ships were rarely anchored at Doha, but rather beached. It was easier to unload cargo or fish, and access to the hulls of the craft for maintenance was more easily afforded. One of the few photographs of Qatar taken during Jassim's lifetime in 1904 shows how the *bateel* and *baqaara* craft were beached and propped up with wooden poles, in upright positions, on the foreshore.

But what of the significant minority of men who wanted nothing whatsoever to do with the sea? There were many men who preferred the ships of the desert. It's estimated that the Emirate had a thousand boats by the end of the nineteenth century, but many more dromedaries. London's representative in Bahrain at the time, Lorimer, reckoned there were around one and a half thousand camels in Qatar. Milk-producing camels were livestock that, together with dates and fish, enriched the local diet. As you might expect, however, there are many types of camel, bred for a variety of tasks ranging from porterage to racing, as well as for meat and milk. They were an extremely valuable resource and the traditional way of measuring wealth and value. Since few roads existed, the camel was also used for local transport, to carry passengers and goods to and from various places around the peninsula and to operate the wells. Women would ride them too, assuming they were correctly seated in a *hawdaj*. Those Bedouin communities that bred camels would also have kept sheep, and we know there was a small trade exporting these to Bahrain.

There was little time for any luxury for the local population. Imports were restricted to the pearling industry's bare necessities; wood was brought in to build boats, ropes for diving and foodstuffs to supplement the home-grown diet. Dates were imported from Hasa, and cloth, mostly cotton bales, was imported from India, usually by way of Bahrain. But despite the hard work necessary for survival, the pace of day-to-day living was slow. No global shipping line ever made regular stops; communication with the outside world was entirely dependent on the local vessels of towns and villages. Before describing how this was to change between 1850 and 1913, we need to describe the political world Jassim found himself in as a young man and the tribal organisation of the peninsula, as well as the policies of his father.

4

TRIBES AND STATE
FORMATION

I WONDER WHAT QATARIS of old would make of
the lettuces and tomatoes harvested in the desert today,
thanks to the marvel of hydroponics and its sister sciences.
In Jassim's time, Qatar had scant agriculture to boast of. The
little it did produce was often pilfered. There were just a
handful of productive date groves in Laqta, Markhiya, Mus-
hairib, Nu'aijah, Sikak, Sakhama and Wakra. The small but
excellent dates they provided, however, were good enough to
warrant harvest-time raids by opportunistic Bedouin tribesmen. Much of neighbouring Hasa suffered similar devasta-
tion, or worse. Land there was far more productive, enough
to stimulate Ottoman reinvasion of the region in 1870. But
farmers frequently abandoned their plantations owing to
almost continuous conflict and unreasonable taxation.

With no central authority in Qatar, the weak were at the
mercy of the strong and the labourers' exertions could be
reduced to mere drudgery in a matter of minutes. Imagine
a farming family's panic as the womenfolk hid and the men
saw the fruits of their labours carried off. The following lines
of verse were written in 1844, and could almost describe the
situation of date farmers in the same year.

A stifled gasp! A dreamy noise, 'The roof is in a flame!'
From out their beds, and to their doors, rush maid and sire and
  dame.
And meet, upon the threshold stone, the gleaming sabres' fall,
And over each black and bearded face the white and crimson
  shawl.
The yell of 'Allah' breaks above the prayer and shriek and roar
Oh, blessed God! The Algerine is Lord of Baltimore.

Of course, the later lines betray the fact that Thomas Osborne
Davis, the Young Irelander, was not describing a British troop raid
on an Irish farm in 1844, but rather an extraordinary Algerian
slave raid on an unsuspecting Irish village some two hundred
years earlier!

Raiding and continual political instability meant that Jassim's
childhood was shorter than most. In the 1840s, neither he nor
his father, Muhammad, was in a position of power over any part
of the peninsula, with the exception of Fuwairit. But any power
Muhammad bin Thani may have held was tenuous. Thousands of
Bahraini and Qatari tribesmen frequented his town in the 1840s,
not to fight him, but to lay siege against each other one month
and engage in battle the next. Despite the difficulties, Muhammad's fortunes endured. To understand why, we must consider the
political and tribal make-up of the region, and the contemporary
power struggles that kept life there anything but boring.

Tribes and political structure

The coastal, revenue-generating communities were relatively
easy to manage, but the Bedouin who roamed inland, with their
camels, sheep and goats, were a different matter. Two-thirds of their
number would only winter in Qatar, attracted by the sparse scrub
that the short rainy season provided. For the rest of the year, they
would keep to the mainland, Hasa and Najd. This was a pattern

established over centuries. Every armed clan had its own area in which to wander, a place where it held grazing rights and access to stone-rimmed wells. This was their *dira*. How Bedouin knew which sections of identical desert belonged to whom is remarkable, and pays tribute to their relationship with an environment they inhabited but never dominated or controlled absolutely.

Each clan was led by a sheikh, whose role it was to resolve disputes and make the important decisions that ensured the welfare of his people. He was not a despot, nor did he enjoy a position in which he could sit back. His right to rule could be challenged by any tribesman, so long as a clan was confident in the challenger's ability. It's important to remember that, in Gulf society, the right to rule was not inherited by the eldest son, but the most capable, so succession was a difficult time for the sheikh's family. Brothers could, and did, end up fighting each other, as happened in the Al Saud family in the 1860s. Often, the ruler needed to placate kinsmen, confident that his siblings would seize on any weakness to dethrone him, as happened in Bahrain to Muhammad bin Khalifa Al Khalifa (with surprising regularity between the 1830s and 1860s). By and large, however, the sheikh's authority was respected and his opinion authoritative. For his part, any leader would always consult before taking major decisions and pay regular stipends to family members out of his income.

Ibn Khaldoun, the great historian and sociologist from Tunis, had observed the dichotomy of sedentary and nomadic life and described the inevitable loss of power that occurred when tribesmen came into regular contact with townsfolk. His fourteenth-century observations on North Africa remained applicable to nineteenth-century Qatar. Two tribes tended to stay in the peninsula's interior throughout the year. The greater threat to security was posed by the Banu Hajir, whose men were not to be dismissed lightly by any potential ruler. Even Ottoman troops stationed in Doha had to pay tribesmen for safe passage through the peninsula's interior. The lack of central authority grew to such an extent that towns would give 'gifts' to the Banu Hajir, who were themselves paying *zakah* to the Wahhabi state in the Najd.

The second clan that remained throughout the year, the Kaban, posed much less of a threat to the stronger coastal communities. The Kaban could not be dominated either, however, as they maintained good relations with their kinsfolk in Hasa and could increase their number quickly if need be. Both Muhammad bin Thani and Jassim, therefore, faced a monumental challenge. The extent of a tribe's *dira* was only as great as its men's ability to defend it. A sheikh who claimed control but couldn't enforce collection of the *zakah* tax from those who roamed within the *dira* was a fraud. And each winter, Qatar was visited by tribes that openly gave their allegiance and tax to the Wahhabi state in the Najd. To tax such tribes twice, if it were possible at all, was to invite war. Local, indigenous sheikhs were in a precarious situation, whereby their power depended on it not being winter.

Of the winter visitors, the Murra and the Ajman proved the biggest, and worst, headaches. Neither tribe remotely felt a need to 'tug a forelock' in the general direction of anyone in Qatar. But there were many other problematic clans too; the Manasir hailed from Trucial Oman and the Naim from both Bahrain and south towards the Trucial coast. Their arrival in October coincided with the end of the pearl season and the date harvest, when more money than usual was hidden under the proverbial mattress. A lot of people in Fuwairit would have been very cautious in their dealings with the tribes that winter drove towards them.

The *hadar*, or settled peoples of Ibn Khaldoun's theory, were made up of around twenty sedentary tribes in the 1840s. The premier division was made up of such clans as the Sultan, the Al Musallam, the Mahandah, the Sudan, the Al bu Kawara, the Hamaydat, the Huwalah, the Al bu Aynain, the Al bin Ali and of course Jassim's own Mi'daad. There were also a Shia Arab tribe known as the Bahraina in Doha. We can have a good guess at their numbers in each town thanks to a British geographic survey completed, oddly enough, in the year of Jassim's birth. Lieutenants Brucks and Guy, whose health suffered terribly on their mission round the Gulf aboard the *Psyche*, made descriptions of tribal strength in most of the villages dotted around the coast. To give a taster, this is what they wrote about Bida: 'This place contains about four hundred Arabs of the Naim, Dawasir and Al bu Kuwara, and is frequented by the Manasir and other wandering tribes.' It is noticeable that no one tried to stop the two British officers from gathering such information, as their research eventually led to the plotting of accurate charts which, in turn, led to the Royal Navy's *Euphrates* steaming up into Iraq in 1836. The steamer's captain, Colonel Chesney, was even told by King William IV: 'Remember, Sir, that the success of England mainly depends upon commerce ... I do not desire war, but if you should be molested, due support shall not be wanting.'

The survey also proved of great use to historians, as it gave the names of other villages with permanent populations. It shows, for example, that Huwaila was a much bigger town than Bida, with more people and more profitable trade. It was able to build its own *ghuri*, or fort, and was protected by 450 fighting men from the Al bu Kuwara. Clearly, Huwaila was not going to be raided very easily, but many of the other settlements were not so fortunate. The survey suggests that such settlements as Lusail, Hadiya, Sumaysma, Dhaayn and Ruwais had barely two hundred men, women and children each. In the absence of any central authority, such towns and villages were governed by local elders who could do little to mount a serious defence against determined opposition.

Conspicuous by its absence, Doha didn't get a mention in Brucks and Guy's survey, possibly because Britain had razed the town to the ground just a few years before they began. In fact, Doha didn't get a decent, written mention by anyone until 1857, when it is lumped in with a description of the natural harbourage offered at Ras Abu Abboud: 'Doha is a town partly walled round, with several towers. It extends eight hundred yards along the beach. The sheikh's house is at a large round tower (with the flagstaff) on the beach, about the centre of the town; to the west of this tower is a small bight, where boats are hauled up to repair.' Such a description suggests that Qatar's east coast had enjoyed substantial growth in the 1830s and 1840s. The same cannot be said for the west coast, where large areas were coming under the authority of Bahraini representatives.

Politicised youth

Life in Qatar in the early 1840s was tense. Key towns on the peninsula were home to political and piratical fugitives attempting to escape British 'justice' or Bahraini jails. The romantic tales of Rahma bin Jabir may have awed a child, but the young Jassim was now confronted in his own town of Fuwairit with a dynastic struggle between the local Isa bin Turaif and the Khalifa of Bahrain. Their dispute would pit thousands of Qatari and Bahraini fighters against each other in some of the bloodiest encounters seen on the peninsula for many centuries. It is a story that would have affected Jassim's political thinking in the years that followed. While it is a complicated story, it needs to be told.

To do justice to bin Turaif's tragic odyssey requires picking up Bahrain's story where we left it in Chapter 1. Following Rahma bin Jabir's spectacular demise in 1826, the embargo on Bahrain had ended. The island's co-rulers, Sheikh Abdullah and his nephew, Sheikh Khalifa, were now in a position to project their power on to neighbouring Qatif, Dammam and the Qatari peninsula. As their strength grew, so did the number of their enemies, and many sought refuge from the duo in the remoter parts of the Qatari peninsula. The historian Habibur Rahman writes: 'Qatar became a breeding ground for their political ambitions and a base for dissident factions of the Al Khalifa family.'

The first of these dissidents to hit British and Persian head-lines was Muhammad bin Khamis, a brother-in-law to the head of the Al bu Aynain tribe in Bida. Muhammad had stabbed a Bah-raini and fled the country to seek the protection of his relatives, particularly their chief, Ali bin Nasir. Bahrain used the incident to send a naval force in 1828 to destroy the Al bu Aynain fort. But the sheikh didn't stop there. Abdullah decided that he would also split the whole tribe up across Fuwairit and Ruwais in the north-east and Zubara in the north-west. The ultimate shame was saved for Ali bin Nasir himself, who was exiled to Wakra without his kinsmen.

Bahrain was all powerful, it seemed. But many of its neigh-bours were keen to see its destruction, particularly Oman. Fortu-nately for the island, disease was to prove an ally. It is amazing how little things can have such dramatic consequences. Clouds pro-tected Kokura from an American atomic bomb in 1945. Painful kidney stones tortured Judge Jeffreys into ordering the execu-tion of 144 Englishmen in two days. But something even smaller would save Bahrain from invasion. The cholera bacterium pre-vented Sultan Sayyid Said's invasion fleet from landing the Omani army on Bahrain's shores in 1828.

Similarly concerned at the apparent growth in Bahraini strength, the Najd's Wahhabi emir, Turki bin Abdullah, decided to pose the island a greater challenge than Oman's abortive attack. He demanded an annual tribute of 40,000 German crowns and the fort at Dammam, which was to be handed over to Rahma bin Jabir's son, Bashir. Sheikh Abdullah temporarily agreed to the terms as he built up local support, before reneging on the deal, along with the Amamara clan in Hasa, and blockading the Wahhabi ports of Qatif and Uqair. What the news of this setback did for Turki's health is anyone's guess, but he died shortly after, leaving his son Faisal to attempt recovery of Dammam in 1835. Bahrain now controlled the Hasa coast, it had seen off Omani and Wahhabi attacks, and now it could turn its attention to Qatar.

In September 1835, Sheikh Abdullah ordered his nephew's sons, Ali and Muhammad, to raid Huwaila and destroy the power and prestige of his son-in-law, Sheikh Isa bin Turaif, who led the Al bin Ali. Bahrain's elite were unconvinced the attack was justified, and two of Sheikh Abdullah's sons even sailed from Muharraq with hundreds of warriors to aid Huwaila's defence against their father. In the town itself, Isa's deputy, Sultan bin Salama, had managed to recruit 2,000 fighters and receive support from the Wahhabi state, including three dozen horsemen and 200 soldiers, as well as dates and rice. Undeterred, Sheikh Abdullah arrived in a deserted Zubara on 3 October 1835 with a thousand men, camels and horses. Marching to Fuwairit, an event Jassim would have personally witnessed as a young ten-year-old boy, Abdullah immediately announced a blockade on Huwaila's harbour and cut off all roads out of town, threatening its people with terrible punishment if they refused to join him.

But Isa bin Turaif delayed fighting a pitched battle, despite his superior numbers. Instead, he put his faith in Sheikh Abdullah's rebellious son Ahmad to negotiate a settlement through the offices of the Sultan of Muscat. To his credit, Ahmad did manage to run the naval blockade on Huwaila, along with bin Salama, on a dark, moonless night on 12 December. The pair arrived at Muscat three days later, however, to discover that the sultan wanted very little to do with the stand-off, though he did send his son to help bring about a political settlement.

There are many occasions when a historian might give his right arm to listen in on a conversation. What did Pope Leo I say to Attila the Hun to prevent his sacking of Rome? Did Ibn Khaldoun really attempt to play the role of brain to Timur's brawn in a bold bid to reunite the fragmented Muslim world? In a more localised, Gulf context, I'd love to have been a fly on the wall at the peace talks between Abdullah and Isa bin Turaif, for the simple reason that the terms are so monumentally one-sided. Isa accepted that Huwaila should not just be evacuated, but actually knocked down, with the entire town's population transferred to Bahrain. Whether any of these terms would have been implemented is doubtful, but the problem is hypothetical, as Abdullah's nephews encouraged the Al bu Kuwara tribe from Fuwairit to attack Huwaila, killing a dependant of bin Turaif and prematurely ending negotiations.

The upshot was that bin Turaif, whether through Bahraini strength or his own poor leadership, took 400 of his kinsmen into exile at Abu Dhabi, with a burning desire to attack Bahraini shipping at the earliest opportunity. But he hadn't appreciated the seismic shifts that were taking place in the mid-1830s. The Gulf was changing, rapidly. There was no way the British authorities would ever allow bin Turaif to flout their maritime peace for the sake of his own private war against Bahrain. As far as the British were concerned, he was in a 'friendly and neutral port' and things were going to have to stay that way. In fact, the government in Bombay was looking to extend its maritime peace, drawing up the 'Operations for the Maritime Truce' in 1835. Halul Island was incorporated into a restrictive no-war zone that extended 10 miles north of Ras Rakkan, at the extreme northern tip of the peninsula.

Isa bin Turaif was not done yet, as we shall see, but in the meantime there were plenty of other dissidents wanting to escape the powers that be in Qatar, a region outside the restrictions of the Trucial coast. One Abu Dhabi outlaw, Jassim Ragragi, who seems by all accounts to have been a rascal of the first order, decided to seek refuge in Wakra, pursued by the East Indiaman *Amherst* (named after an incompetent governor-general of India whose wife lent her name to a species of pheasant in Bedfordshire). The sight of a British warship was enough to convince Ali bin Nasir, who was expelled to Wakra by Abdullah, that it would be a good time to leave, and he promptly sailed to join bin Turaif at Abu Dhabi in March 1838. Sensing the beginning of a bigger anti-Bahraini alliance, bin Turaif now decided to flirt with Egyptian power.

Muhammad Ali, an Albanian who theoretically took orders from the Sublime Porte but actually ruled Egypt, Syria and Arabia's eastern shores by himself in the late 1830s, had transferred command of his troops in Najd in May 1838 to Khurshid Pasha. Khurshid had set up his headquarters at Anaiza, roughly two hundred miles to the north-east of Riyadh. He spent the summer there, much to British concern, consolidating the Egyptian hold on the country and building up a supply depot. Reinforcements of troops, about two thousand men, were sent to him, and with these he set out in late September for Riyadh. Shortly afterwards, Khurshid began to advance eastwards into Hasa. Ahead of him, he sent messengers to the sheikhs of Bahrain and Kuwait, informing them of his advance and asking them to provide supplies for his troops when they reached the Gulf coast.

For bin Turaif to dangle the name Khurshid Pasha in front of British officials would no doubt have garnered their most earnest attention. Egyptian influence, already threatening to overcome Ottoman power, would jeopardise British interests. Thus, a Captain Edmunds, Assistant Political Resident in the Gulf, was sent to reconcile Bahrain's Sheikh Abdullah with bin Turaif, after accepting two promises. The first was bin Turaif's word that he would end contact with Khurshid Pasha, and the second that he would stop harassing the Bahraini pearling fleet. Unbeknown to the British during that May of 1839, however, Bahrain had not been waiting idly for an imposed British compromise and had met Muhammad Effendi, a secret agent of Khurshid Pasha, in Hasa. In fact, Abdullah had gone one step farther, agreeing to pay Egypt some three thousand German crowns a year on the understanding that the Egyptian governor and general would support Sheikh Abdullah's plans to control north-eastern Qatar.

Bin Turaif had been outmanoeuvred once again; Sheikh Abdullah had clearly undermined any alliance bin Turaif might possibly propose with Khurshid. But the deal wasn't as clever as it first appeared. Paying tribute to Egypt went down like a lead balloon among Sheikh Abdullah's clansmen, and a large portion of his tribe decided to quit the island altogether. Although opposition increased, Sheikh Abdullah pushed on with his plans and landed troops on Qatar's eastern coast in June 1839, asking Muhammad Effendi to attack one of his own dissenting clansmen. Khurshid Pasha's reputation was done immeasurable harm after the troops he sent were repulsed. Abdullah was forced to retreat, and 2,000 of the Al bu Kuwara, who had once supported the Bahraini sheikh, emigrated from Qatar to the island of Kharg in protest. Most of these tribesmen had been based in Fuwairit, and their departure meant that Muhammad bin Thani now became the undisputed head of the town.

Emboldened by Abdullah's reversal of fortunes, Isa bin Turaif now insisted the British back his plans to resettle his entire clan in either Bida or Wakra, and dropped a compromise proposal of re-establishing his people on Kharg Island. Proposal followed counterproposal; some even included bin Turaif's suggestion that Britain govern the whole of Bahrain with the help of his tribe and dissatisfied factions of the Al bu Kuwara, who had abandoned Abdullah. Hennell, the British Political Resident, spelled out his reluctance to get involved in a letter to the Sultan of Muscat. 'The reasons which had principally led me to oppose the hostile views of Isa bin Turaif against Shaikh Abdullah, were firstly the circumstance that his so doing would promote the views of Khushid Pasha in his then projected attack on Bahrain, and secondly … if the Al bin Ali effected an independent establishment for themselves upon the Qatar Coast then dispute with Shaikh Abdullah would resolve into a mere local quarrel in which I did not see any call for our interference.' In short, Britain was worried about an Egyptian takeover of Bahrain, and that a new independent statelet inside Qatar and run by bin Turaif might just promote such a chain of events.

Worried by developments, Abu Dhabi's Sheikh Khalifa bin Shakhbout now began to put real pressure on bin Turaif to leave.

Khalifa, who had only just recovered from a power struggle with his brother Sultan, faced his own challenges, most important of which was a growing exodus of residents to a newly established Dubai. Bin Turaif, not willing to outstay his welcome or spend any more money, was also keen to leave, and told Hennell that he was going to take the Al bin Ali to Wakra. The British official immediately sensed that the joining of the Al bu Aynain, under Sheikh Ali bin Nasir, and the Al bin Ali, under bin Turaif, was a recipe for a breakdown in his own relations with Bahrain. Hennell made a show of asking Bombay for their opinion on allowing settlement of Wakra, even writing that bin Turaif had 'afforded the most satisfactory proofs that he promises not only power, but the desire to suppress and punish all proceedings of a piratical character'. Sheikh Abdullah somehow came to know of the plan and made a deal with Sheikh Khalifa to harry bin Turaif as soon as he arrived in Wakra from the south while Bahrain planned to attack from the north.

Outmanoeuvred once more, bin Turaif acknowledged his second diplomatic defeat on visiting Hennell aboard the *Clive* in December 1839. He now dropped the idea of returning to his beloved Qatar, and proposed settling the Al bin Ali on Qais. A small island in the Gulf, Qais is the last land of any size before a ship can reach the Strait of Hormuz, as one sails from Iraq along the Persian coast. Its happy situation made it an ideal maritime stronghold of the medieval seafaring world, and it even took the place of Siraf, the famous emporium of the Abbasid period, as the main centre of commerce between Iraq, Iran and India. The last Islamic geographer to use the great library at Baghdad before its destruction, Yaqut al-Hamawi,★ had visited Qais several times on his commercial travels in the thirteenth century and described its important location and murderous climate.

Bin Turaif's choice of Qais met with British approval; in fact

★ Yaqut al-Hamawi (1179–1229) started life as a Greek slave in the Syrian town of Hama, but ended up a top Islamic scholar in Baghdad.

Hennell jumped at the idea. He didn't do so out of consideration for conditions on the island or the livelihood it might provide the men who were to live on it. He agreed because Qais fell within the boundary line laid down by London as the limit of Arab maritime hostilities. The British would now guarantee that any migrants on Qais would be free of fear of molestation from either Sheikh Abdullah or Abu Dhabi's Banu Yas. By February 1840, the Al bin Ali were safely transferred and the immediate consequences of Hennell's decision became obvious to him.

A British attack

While the futures of bin Turaif and Ali bin Nasir had remained undetermined in Abu Dhabi, a semblance of order had been maintained in Bida and Wakra by the Sudan tribe, headed by Salman bin Nasir al-Suwaidi. But once it was clear that the respective heads of the Al bin Ali and Al bu Aynain would not be returning any time soon, Bida became a sanctuary for every kind of undesirable troublemaker in the Gulf. Men such as Jassim Ragragi had taken to inviting the brightest and best of the Gulf's criminal world. Ships were being raided with increasing audacity and all fingers pointed to Bida, a miniature version of the Caribbean's Tortuga, if you will. Last to join this piratical brotherhood was another Abu Dhabi outlaw, who went by the name of Ghuleta. Their unlawful operations might have continued a little while longer were it not for this new arrival. Unfortunately for Bida, Ghuleta seemed incapable of appreciating that there were some ships it would be better not to board. Stealing a Basra-based ship under British protection while moored in the Persian port of Bandar Dillam was the final straw. The Resident's ship, HMS *Clive*, made for Bida and anchored off the coast in full view of the entire populace. The ship's captain, A. H. Nott, invited Sudan chief Salman bin Nasir aboard for a chat and the situation deteriorated rapidly.

The problem for Salman bin Nasir, who had managed to imprison Ghuleta, Ragragi and the other ringleaders by the end of 1840, was that he considered himself a victim of the pirate gang just as much as the British. He felt no compulsion to pay any compensation for piracy that had been committed along neighbouring coasts. Hennell welcomed the gang's arrest but demanded the whole community of Bida accept ultimate responsibility and pay a fine of 300 German crowns on the pirates' behalf by the end of February 1841 at the latest. Salman was in a quandary. First and most obviously, he didn't have 300 German crowns. Secondly, it had taken all his efforts to finally capture the pirate gang, who had made his own people, the Sudan, suffer much more than the British ever had. No one likes living with pirates. Lastly, of course, Salman was unaccustomed to being held responsible for the crimes of people not under his protection. The British had no concept of tribal justice, which necessitated returning criminals to their own tribes for punishment.

But with all the inevitability of a Greek tragedy, HMS *Coote*, HMS *Sesostris* and HMS *Tigris* anchored off Bida on 25 February 1841. Commodore Brucks communicated his intention either to pick up the cash, and the ship stolen from Bandar Dillam, or to bombard the town until he was able to do so. Salman handed over the ship, but declined to accept responsibility for handing over any monies, writing back to the commodore:

> Your demand is not a just one. Your business belongs to
> Ragragi who is no subject of mine. He is of the Banu Yas
> and [Abu Dhabi's] Sheikh Khalifa bin Shakhbout. If it could
> be proved that I have gained anything from Ragragi's acts of
> piracy, I would return the money twenty-fold. The boat in
> which he committed his crimes was from Ras al-Khaima,
> which I impounded along with the ones he has plundered.
> He himself has since escaped. In doing this I thought I was
> performing a good act which all would approve of. Ragragi's
> boat is here and at your disposal. When my men searched his

vessels they were empty and deserted. Enquire into the business and do justice. If I am in fault, enforce your demand. If I am right, do not harm me.

The newly promoted Commodore Brucks was not there to investigate, however, but to collect. Rejecting Salman's note, he ordered his squadron to open fire on Bida the next morning, destroying the fort and the mud-brick houses built around it. If anything can be said in defence of the British action, it is only that at least this time the reason for the attack was made plain and warning given. (In 1821, neither the Al bu Aynain chief, Buhur bin Jubran, nor a single one of his people had any idea why the East Indiaman *Vestal* had burned the town down, as the British Political Resident admitted a few months later.) In any case, the Sudan chief had to stop the shelling and hide his rage as he agreed to hand over his people's wealth: 42 silver bracelets, one sword, a silver hair ornament, four pairs of gold earrings, two pairs of silver earrings, two daggers and nine bead necklaces. It seems that it was the Sudan women who paid the ultimate price of piracy, losing husbands, homes and jewellery – their only financial asset.

Having 'restored order' at Bida, Brucks was keen to get his hands on Ragragi and steered a course up the coast towards Fuwairit, where he expected his quarry to take refuge. At the same time, Brucks urged Sheikh Abdullah to write a letter on his behalf to the chief of the town. Abdullah obliged and wrote, on 27 March 1841, to a Sheikh Muhammad bin Thani, head of the Mi'daad and chief of Fuwairit, asking him not to harbour Ragragi or afford him any protection.

This was noteworthy. It was the first reference in a British source to Jassim's father, Sheikh Muhammad. It was also the first document to recognise Al Thani authority over the town that had also been home to other Banu Tamim clans such as the Al bu Kuwara. Jassim's career had begun. His father was the rec- ognised head of an important town. He was now part of the political order. The misfortunes of Isa bin Turaif were yet to haunt

Fuwairit, but Jassim had learnt his first lessons: the fractious nature of tribal rivalries and the error of relying on regional powers such as Britain or Egypt.

5

JASSIM'S FATHER

MUCH IS KNOWN about Muhammad bin Thani as a politician and diplomat. He laid the foundations which would one day permit Jassim to establish an independent, sovereign Qatar. But what of Muhammad bin Thani, the man and father? Here things become a little more uncertain, for William Gifford Palgrave is the only man known to have jotted down some fairly sketchy impressions of the sheikh. The language he chose to employ was often condescending and arrogant. He would describe Qatar in 1863 as 'rubbish' and its houses as 'rubbishy'. What would such a man be likely to say, then, about the peninsula's most prominent leader?

Before finding out, keep in mind that Palgrave had a complex and controversial character. A would-be Jesuit missionary, he could barely tolerate the company of those he was trying to convert. On his return to England, he renounced his Catholicism and spent two years writing up *A Year's Journey through Central and Eastern Arabia*. There was something of the orientalist Richard Burton in him, but without the sparkling intellect. Later travellers in the Arab world, such as Harry St John Philby, known to his Arab friends as Sheikh Abdullah, were of the opinion that

Palgrave was an outright liar. His fame is, perhaps in part, due to a talented and influential father. Sir Francis Palgrave founded Britain's Public Record Office and married well. Nevertheless, William provides our only description of Sheikh Muhammad's appearance and character.

'Bin Thani, the governor of Bida, is indeed generally acknowledged for head of the entire province,' he wrote. 'He is a shrewd wary old man, slightly corpulent, and renowned for prudence and good-humoured easiness of demeanour, but close-fisted and a hard customer at a bargain.' The description goes on. Muhammad had more 'the air of a pearl-merchant than a tribal chieftain', but that may have had something to do with his style of dress. 'He wore a Bengali turban, of the date of Siraj al-Dawla [who died in 1757], to judge by its dingy appearance; his robe was an overdress which a Damascene grocer would have been ashamed to display out of doors.' Despite Palgrave's scorn, it is clear Muhammad was a hard-working, hands-on ruler rather than a ruby-encrusted raja of some East Indian province. The Brit abroad also reveals that by 1863 Muhammad bin Thani had control over Bida as well as Fuwairit, with the power to tax and collect revenue.

Al Thani rise to power

Muhammad had become a major political player in the Gulf at the very beginning of the 1840s. This was an achievement and a testament to his acute diplomatic skills. The 1840s were one of Qatar's most bloody and unstable decades for a century. Bahraini dynastic disputes were spilling over on to the peninsula with increasing frequency and loss of life. Meanwhile, Britain's Royal Navy had grown confident in her unchallenged strength in the Gulf. Possessing the only steamships in the region, Queen Victoria's navy held considerable power over all things maritime. So it was that any local leader whose political fortunes rose in that decade must have known a thing or two. To understand how the

Al Thani grew in strength, we must complete the story of Sheikh Isa bin Turaif.

In 1841, many more clansmen from the Al bin Ali and Al bu Aynain had left Qatar to join the exiled bin Turaif on Qais Island. A potential invasion force was clearly gathering to attack Bahrain, which was in the throes of civil war. Both Bahraini factions wanted to be sure of support in Qatar, and pressure was growing on Muhammad bin Thani and other local leaders to choose a side. The alternatives were equally appalling. Should the Al Thani back the veteran but intransigent Sheikh Abdullah Al Khalifa or his inexperienced great-nephew Muhammad bin Khalifa? The young Jassim, around eighteen at this time, wouldn't have backed either. He was far more impressed by men such as Faisal bin Turki, who was working hard with his Wahhabi confederates to build up the Second Saudi State.

Over the course of the next three years, both Al Khalifa factions would take turns at establishing their forces in Dammam, Khor Hasan and Zubara. Neither party was prepared to compromise. Both sides wanted absolute power and both would do battle at the drop of a hat. For example, in 1843, fighting flared up when Muhammad bin Khalifa stopped the marriage of a young Muharraq beauty to one of Abdullah's sons. Eventually, Abdullah's old age began to tell and his grand-nephew had the better of their encounters, especially once bin Turaif and Bashir bin Rahma decided to take his side in the conflict. Even Abdullah's sons recognised the end was nigh and joined the opposition. Muhammad's hold over Bahrain was almost complete. Bin Turaif brought his clan back from Qais to Bida in triumph, once the pearling season closed. He immediately replaced the shell-shocked leader of the Sudan, Salman bin Nasir, sending him and his clan into exile in Lingeh, their prestige in tatters following the British attack two years earlier.

Characteristically, Abdullah refused to admit defeat. He attempted to build an alliance with the Saudi state in the Najd himself, following the hurried withdrawal of Egyptian forces in 1840. Fresh out of a Cairene jail, Faisal bin Turki Al Saud was initially prepared to consider such an alliance. But doing time in Muhammad Ali's Egypt had matured his political sagacity. (He was to rule adroitly for twenty years and with increasing strength.) Faisal recognised a lost cause when he saw one and ended military cooperation by asking the venerable Sheikh Abdullah to leave Dammam. Unfortunately, Faisal's wisdom was not contagious. Isa bin Turaif had never recognised Bahraini authority in Qatar, it was a well-known fact, but he had helped Muhammad bin Khalifa defeat his great-uncle. Rather than keeping Bahrain's new ruler as a friend, or just keeping quiet as two Khalifa factions fought each other, he constantly attempted to get involved. He not so secretly encouraged Muscat to attempt another invasion of Bahrain in 1843. The plan was to no avail; Muscat was not interested. But news of the instigator's identity reached the ears of both Khalifa factions. Impressively, bin Turaif had managed to do what no one else could have. He had soured relations with both Khalifa factions at the same time, a move he would regret to his death, which was fast and fatefully approaching.

Muhammad bin Thani showed a much greater appreciation of the situation, and had strongly supported Muhammad bin Khalifa's claim to power over all of Bahrain. He had permitted ships to be stationed in Fuwairit after Abdullah managed to capture Manama briefly that year, reasoning that if one Bahraini sheikh was to fight another, then neither would be fighting him. Muhammad was not supporting Muhammad bin Khalifa out of conviction and would not allow Jassim to take part in the attack on Sheikh Abdullah in Manama. Jassim too was unimpressed by the merit of Muhammad bin Khalifa's claim to rule, but he did wish to weaken the hold Bahrain enjoyed over western Qatar. For this reason, the young Jassim rashly allowed some of his kinsmen from the Mi'daad to settle at Bida in conspicuous support of bin Turaif. The whole of the Al bu Kuwara, under Muhammad bin

Said, had also joined forces with the Al bin Ali chief, as had his brother-in-law Ali bin Nasir in Wakra. But Muhammad bin Thani was wise to bide his time in Fuwairit, delaying any move to join forces with Bida. Bin Turaif's leadership skills were highly questionable, as his years in exile had proved. As far as Muhammad bin Thani was concerned, there was no hurry to fight in Bahrain. History was to prove him right. Trouble was coming to Qatar soon enough; there was no need to go looking for it.

It is odd that the British did not oppose bin Turaif's appropriation of Bida in 1843, considering the lengths to which their Political Resident had gone to prevent it. The reason may have something to do with Hennell enjoying six months' leave in Britain. He had been deputised by a 23-year-old lieutenant, Arnold Burrowes Kemball, who lacked his superior's experienced caution. (Kemball was photographed in 1860 by the young French aristocrat Camille Silvy, complete with his Victorian sideburns and waistcoat, a dead ringer for Prince Albert – but without the hair.) Kemball welcomed the turn of events in Bida, convinced that with a new population came an opportunity to wipe the slate clean and improve relations. He felt the Al bin Ali would tackle any piracy problems with alacrity. He was also pleased that bin Turaif's men were now, as he put it, 'within the Arabian side of the restrictive line'. And for almost three years it looked as if this young man's optimism was well founded. The Al bin Ali were at last settled; Sheikh Abdullah was out of the picture. In November 1843, bin Turaif had paid an official visit, meeting up with Sheikh Muhammad bin Khalifa and his supporters in Bahrain. The Al bin Ali chief had even offered his services in stamping out the continuing resistance that Abdullah offered from the Hasawi coast. It was an unprecedented period of calm.

But things didn't last. This was no peace, merely an absence of war. As Muhammad bin Khalifa became more confident of his position, he once again began to interfere in Qatar. Bin Turaif was alarmed to discover that Bahrain was rebuilding the fort at Zubara.

He was aware too of frequent Bahraini visits to Fuwairit. The Al Khalifa were showering their unwanted attentions on northeast Qatar. Most importantly of all, bin Turaif was afraid that his beloved home town of Huwaila would fall into Bahraini hands once again. He decided, therefore, to seek out a military alliance with the very man who had caused his many years of exile in the first place, the father-in-law who had caused his people's exodus to Qais. He sought out Sheikh Abdullah. Restarting the Bahraini civil war was surprisingly simple, but this time bin Turaif was fighting on the other side, and openly declared his support for Muhammad bin Khalifa's arch-enemy. This was exactly the kind of reckless decision which made Muhammad bin Thani wary of throwing in his lot with the Al bin Ali. Jassim would have learned a valuable lesson.

Bin Turaif's dramatic change of policy caught Muhammad bin Khalifa by surprise. News of it coincided, however, with the arrival of a British naval squadron patrolling the Gulf in November 1847. The Bahraini sheikh made straight for the flagship, commanded by a Captain William Lowe, to let it be known that the maritime peace was about to broken. Muhammad embellished the facts considerably, as Lowe heard how Sheikh Abdullah, based on Qais all these years following his expulsion from Dammam, was plotting an invasion with the Al bin Ali chief. Their plan was to attack with hundreds of ships post-haste. Knowing it would provoke a reaction, Sheikh Muhammad added that Bahrain had no choice but to defend itself with a fleet of its own *baghla*s, each one bearing men armed to the teeth.

Muhammad bin Khalifa played the part perfectly. Lowe left their meeting, that 2 November, irritated by Bida's new alliance with Abdullah and the prospect of a major sea battle after four years of calm. His career depended on the serenity of the shipping lanes; Lowe was determined that there should be no disturbance to trade. Without waiting to ascertain whether the story so expertly spun was accurate, the captain wrote to bin Turaif informing him that the Royal Navy would seize any of his vessels found to be carrying tribesmen or weapons anywhere in the Gulf. Rather than responding to the British, bin Turaif demanded that Muhammad return the vessels he had stolen from Abdullah. This hasty response allowed Muhammad to play his trump card. Writing to Lowe on 4 November, he used bin Turaif's response as proof that an invasion was imminent and that the ships the Al bin Ali chief spoke of were to be used for 'an act of perfidy. He [bin Turaif] has contacted Abdullah bin Ahmad, and his son Mubarak, and the others who are with him, of the Banu Hajir tribe. His object is to invade my territory, and subject the people of Qatar who are my dependants to himself.'

Bin Turaif attempted to reason with Hennell, insisting it was Bahrain which threatened Qatar's territorial integrity.

> We write to inform you with regard to Muhammad bin Khalifa and his brother Ali, who have acted treacherously towards us in return for the good, which as you know, we did them. They launched six *baghla*s and two *bateel*s, when the captain arrived at Bahrain and put a stop to their proceedings. The captain also wrote an interdictory letter to us, and we desisted from all hostile preparations. Subsequently Ali bin Khalifa put to sea with warships and three boats, and cast anchor at Fuwairit. We know not what his object may be, but you are aware that Huwaila is in our country, and we fear but he should take it. Such is the way in which they harass and annoy us in exchange for the services we rendered there.

Hennell didn't reply. Bin Turaif was convinced Bahrain and Britain had come to some arrangement. There was no time to be lost. With scant preparation or time to recruit large numbers of men, he risked the destruction of his fleet on 7 November to land men at Fuwairit. His haste meant he could muster only 400, but bin Turaif was hopeful other tribesmen would rally to his cause. Muhammad bin Thani's heart may have been with him, and he welcomed bin Turaif into the town. But he knew that this was not an army to fight a British-backed Bahrain. There was only one way the coming confrontation would end. Sure enough, Muhammad bin Khalifa ordered the fleet to land his 1,000-strong army at Zubara, where it could be supported with cavalry and ample supplies. The men would then march across the top of the peninsula and fall upon Fuwairit. As the military build-up intensified, the British authorities dispatched several warships, including the eighteen-gun sloop *Elphinstone*, to blockade Bida and prevent Turaif from receiving reinforcements or supplies by sea.

On 13 November, Hennell made a show of attempting to stop any maritime confrontation with letters to both belligerents. The missive reveals that he had no interest in preventing battle on land. 'It is not my intention to interfere between you so long as hostilities are confined to Bahrain and Qatar, but any of your vessels found cruising in the Persian side of the Gulf or elsewhere without the restrictive line will be immediately seized by our vessels of war.' But this was not the case at all. It is clear Lowe's orders were to stop Qatari ships only. Just two days after Hennell's warning, Ali bin Khalifa landed at Al Khor with some five hundred men under his command. His ships must have sailed past British vessels anchored in Muharraq's harbour. The Bahraini governors at Hasa and Qatif, Ahmad al-Sudairi and bin Uthman, had also sent men and supplies by sea. Muhammad bin Khalifa now landed with the remainder of his forces, leading an army of just under two thousand men.

In the opposing camp, the Al bin Ali and their supporters had managed to recruit just 600 soldiers and no cavalry at all. Nor was there any hope of more troops from Qais or Bida, so long as a second Royal Naval squadron patrolled the Qatari coastline. It was clear to both Muhammad bin Thani and his son that the battle was lost before it was begun, and neither wanted to see their town come under siege. Discretion being the better part of valour, and urging bin Turaif to negotiate, neither Muhammad nor Jassim took part in the Battle of Fuwairit on 17 November 1847.

The fight was spectacularly short lived. Bin Turaif was killed almost immediately, along with 80 of his kinsmen. The resolve of the hastily assembled coalition withered within the hour. Satisfied that the Al Thani had not joined the fray, Muhammad bin Khalifa marched on Bida with the intention of giving the Al bin Ali a lesson history would never forget. Once again, Britain allowed Bahraini warships to pass down the eastern Qatari coast and raze Bida to the ground for the third time in 30 years. Its people were transported en masse back to Bahrain for closer scrutiny. Bin Turaif's impotent ally, Sheikh Abdullah, fled to Nabend on the Persian coast, where he lived out the rest of his life. Sheikh Abdullah's son Mubarak marched to the Najd with the 200 men he had failed to lead into battle. Bin Turaif's children were exiled to Qais once more, and Ali bin Khalifa was instructed to remain as Bahrain's representative. This was without doubt the lowest point in Qatar's bid for independence; all leadership had been eliminated. It was into this power vacuum that the Al Thani now stepped. Their time had arrived.

The Battle of Fuwairit was a turning point. Muhammad bin Thani's patience and good sense were to pay dividends. By remaining neutral throughout the ill-prepared conflict, by surviving the worst of the storm, Muhammad bin Thani had held on to Fuwairit, Sulaiman al-Suwaidi had regained Bida once more, and Ali bin Nasir was undisputed leader in Wakra. The destruction wrought by Muhammad bin Khalifa had, ironically, helped forge the idea of a Qatari identity. A poor leader, bin Turaif had nevertheless fought and died to keep the peninsula free of foreign interference. The effort was not lost on the sheikhs who remained. Jassim was to learn from bin Turaif's mistake. He realised that an independent Qatar could not be created through the strength and alliances of one tribe, but rather through a union of tribes backed by a powerful ally.

The Wahhabi opportunity

When Faisal bin Turki left Egypt, he had demanded the 'rebel' Sheikh Abdullah leave Dammam in exchange for annual tribute from Abdullah's rival and grand-nephew, Muhammad. Faisal was in need of money quickly if he were to stand any chance of re-establishing the Saud–Wahhabi state. By the late 1840s, he had been largely successful and had taken absolute control of the Najd and Hasa provinces. Faisal's growing strength and political influence were impossible to ignore. The Qatari peninsula had no natural barrier to invasion from Hasa and the province's coastal town of Uqair was a mere 30 miles from Bahrain, an ideal location from which to launch an invasion. This unhappy geographic proximity maintained regional tensions right up until the beginning of the 21st century. But Bahrain's fleet was well over a thousand ships strong. Faisal's army was far superior in strength and number, but transporting it to the island of Bahrain was fraught with danger. Bahrain was the shark to the Wahhabi elephant, both powerful in their own element.

The shift in regional power prompted a scramble for new political alliances. Muhammad bin Thani would have been keenly aware that any additional agreement between Faisal and Muhammad bin Khalifa would prove highly detrimental to Fuwairit and Qatar, depriving the peninsula of political leverage. There was ample historical precedent to goad him into action. Just a decade earlier, when Egyptian forces were allied with the Al Khalifa in Hasa, an invasion force was on the verge of attacking Jabir bin Nasir's Naim tribe for refusal to pay tribute to Bahrain. Muhammad needed to form an alliance with Faisal before Muhammad bin Khalifa, if he were to stand any chance of manipulating Wahhabi strength and ridding Qatar of Bahraini interference once and for all.

The first step in realising such an alliance was to move closer to Hasa. Maintaining control over Fuwairit, Muhammad, Jassim and the Al Thani moved to Doha in 1849. The town had an excellent natural harbour and was still deserted following Bahraini reprisals three years earlier. Their authority and prestige were growing as the tribe successfully defended its expansion. When the Al bin Ali survivors eventually returned to Bida, not one of them made any pretence at leadership. Muhammad bin Thani was the man with whom all officials dealt. And when yet another Abu Dhabi pirate sought refuge in Qatar after stealing a Kuwaiti ship, Hennell contacted Muhammad for restitution, referring to him as Sheikh of Doha and Fuwairit. The Al Thani chief was no longer just the leader of the Mi'daad now; he had also taken the Al bu Kuwara under his wing too, along with the few Al Musallam, Sulaithi and Manai tribesmen in Doha. (The town was right next to Bida, just 400 yards away in fact, and the two settlements would soon be joined for ever.) This unity and recognition of authority brought safety, which encouraged the arrival of migrant workers. An increasing population brought increasing returns to the town's pearling revenue. Muhammad now cut quite the figure in society and was in a far stronger position to contact the Wahhabi emir, Faisal. He had something to offer. Qatar's east coast was under his control; what was needed now was to remove Bahrain's aspiration to suzerainty.

An opportunity came in February 1851. Muhammad discovered that Faisal was on the move, leading an army from the Najd to an oasis called Jooda, between Qatif and Hasa. Tens of hundreds of men were reported to be with him. It was clear the Wahhabi emir was attempting an invasion. But of whom? Sheikh Muhammad's thoughts must have raced as he considered a myriad of possibilities. There was only one chance to get this right; Muhammad bin Khalifa did not yet consider the Al Thani as an enemy and Wahhabi intentions were unclear. What might he demand from Qatar? Could Faisal be persuaded to use Doha as a springboard to attack Bahrain? Would it be possible to bring in Sheikh Abdullah's exiled sons, now led by Mubarak bin Abdullah? The British political agent, Hennell, was asking equally searching questions, and wrote for some answers. Faisal at last explained his intentions. 'The Bahrain sheikhs have squandered their property on my subjects so that they might attach them to their own side while excusing themselves from paying me tribute.'

As more details became clear, Muhammad must have realised he was about to play host to yet another army that could not be denied entry to Doha for long, but which might be distracted into invading Bahrain. He needed to buy some time, and turned to Jassim to delay Faisal while he attempted to gather the ousted Khalifa family on Qais to propose the invasion of Bahrain to the Wahhabi emir. Demonstrating incredible strength of character and loyalty to his father (he was sympathetic to the Wahhabi cause throughout his life), a 24-year-old Jassim led horse and foot soldiers through the streets of Doha and Bida, flying a red Qatari banner, towards the vanguard of Faisal's army, led by a truly ferocious Bedouin warrior called Musa'id. That Musa'id perished on the end of Jassim's lance was enough to ensure his own personal prestige as a respected warrior, but his self-confidence was no doubt boosted as his men recognised his genuine leadership skills too. Faisal's vanguard was driven back to camp at Mesaimeer. He had bought the time his father needed with utmost credit, and his father did not squander the window of opportunity Jassim had provided. At his instigation, the rebel Mubarak bin Abdullah Al Khalifa informed Faisal directly that he could bring men and transport ships to Doha for a proposed invasion of Bahrain and that arrangements had already been made with Muhammad bin Thani. If any additional incentive were needed, Sheikh Abdullah's son further promised an annual tribute of 10,000 German crowns once the Wahhabis were safely installed in Bahrain. Faisal agreed and marched his forces towards Doha to prepare.

As he drew near to the town that May, Sheikh Muhammad bin Khalifa's brother Ali sailed out to Zakhnuniya island, opposite Faisal's camp, on 2 May, and suggested a delegate be sent to negotiate, and that Bahrain was prepared to offer a year's tribute and all arrears in order to avert war. The reply demanded that Ali parley in person, to which he responded: 'If you are pleased to make peace on the terms already proposed, good. Otherwise there is no further necessity to wait longer for us. You can go where you like and we will be there before you.'

Muhammad bin Thani's time for consideration was over. If he wanted an alliance with Faisal bin Turki, it was now or never. The Sheikh of Bahrain's own brother was resident in Bida and would soon be asking why Jassim had undertaken only a few preliminary skirmishes. The situation was more critical than many in Doha realised. Concerned that Bahrain might fall, the British were planning for the total annihilation of Doha in a bid to stop its use by Faisal as a base for operations. The only people in town who knew of this development were Muhammad and Jassim. They were told by a suspicious Ali bin Khalifa that Bahrain would assist the Royal Navy in razing Doha to the ground should any hint of disloyalty to Bahrain manifest itself. More pressure was exerted on Doha's chief with news that Abu Dhabi, now led by Sheikh Said bin Tahnun, wanted to prevent Faisal from entering Doha at all costs and was sending ships and men to aid in its defence.

Just two days before Faisal's arrival, Sheikh Ali bin Khalifa returned to Bida with the intention of overseeing the town's defences and pressing as many men into service as possible. Before he could begin, however, Ali was called to a meeting with Muhammad bin Thani. What was said must have shaken him to the core. Ali was told that Bida, Doha and Fuwairit would not resist Faisal's army, and that, on the contrary, a message of welcome had already been sent to the Wahhabi emir. As they spoke, Al Thani tribesmen were busy removing Khalifa sympathisers from the Burj al-Mah, the most strategic fort that controlled entry into Bida and access to its wells. It was also the fort where Ali was resident. Muhammad had made his decision and there was no going back. He felt certain that now was the moment to end Bahraini intimidation. He would use Wahhabi strength to counter the British–Bahraini alliance.

After making his intentions clear, Muhammad bin Thani demonstrated his chivalrous nature, assuring Ali he was not a prisoner and was free to leave, advising him to do so before Faisal arrived. He permitted Hamdan bin Tahnun of Abu Dhabi to return home too.

Faisal was pleased to find his army welcomed into Doha, though he was angered by Muhammad's decision to let Ali go. Nevertheless, the first stage of his plan had succeeded without so much as a shot being fired. Mubarak bin Abdullah had also kept his promise, reporting that he was busy gathering vessels to transport the invasion force. Preparations seemed to be proceeding well. The mood was not as cheerful in Bahrain. News of Muhammad bin Thani's decision to abandon his usual caution went down very poorly. Muhammad bin Khalifa decided upon a naval blockade of Doha and looked to the British for support in preventing a possible secondary attack from Qais. Just to be safe, he also matched the offer of 10,000 German crowns a year for Abdullah's descendants if they agreed to stay away. He even suggested to Hennell that Bahrain become a British protectorate once Faisal and his new allies had been defeated. Hennell was unimpressed by the offer, decided against shelling Doha once Faisal had entered it and initially seemed resigned to the fact that Bahrain would fall. Such a scenario seemed likely before one Colonel Justin Sheil involved himself in affairs.

Sheil is a fascinating character. An Irishman born near Waterford and educated at Stonyhurst, he served in the Bengal Infantry and was present at the siege of Bhurtpore in 1826. Promoted up through the ranks, he was described by his friends as 'sensible and well-informed' with a temper that was 'mild and conciliatory'. Some credited him, apocryphally, I believe, with ending torture in Persia, inducing the Shah to abandon his predilection for cutting off prisoners' heads as an afternoon indulgence, but only after their eyes had been gouged out. Sheil's other acquaintances weren't quite so admiring. The Right Honourable Member for Poole in England, H. D. Seymour, described the colonel in very different terms at the House of Commons. 'He is a bully, and his policy is a bullying policy.' Whatever the truth, Sheil was of the opinion that any Qatari–Wahhabi attack on Bahrain would benefit only the Ottoman Empire. His foresight was truly remarkable, and the Horse Guards military command was convinced. The British insisted something had to be done. Muhammad bin Khalifa needed to be saved.

Hennell sent a short, polite letter to Muhammad bin Thani which began with the promising words: 'It is not the intention of the British Government to interfere in the quarrel.' But the sting, as so often is the case, was in the tail. 'You cannot be permitted to place your maritime resources at the disposal of a foreign power, and therefore you are interdicted, under pain of incurring the severe displeasure of the British Government, from employing your vessels for the invasion of Bahrain.' Hennell was saying, in effect, that Faisal was welcome to invade the island of Bahrain, just so long as he didn't use any ships to get there. Hennell also sent HMS *Tigris* to prevent any troopships from leaving Qais, though some had managed to slip out of port before her arrival.

Meanwhile, Muhammad bin Khalifa was intent on mounting a strong defence. Disappointed at the British decision not to flatten Doha, he took matters into his own hands and ordered the blockade of Qatif. His plan was to prevent any ship sailing that could possibly be used to transport Faisal's army to the Bahraini coast. Smarting from the Doha debacle, Ali bin Khalifa was happy to take command of eleven warships and 800 armed men. He had no sooner arrived at Qatif in July when he came upon eighteen transport ships that had sailed from Qais before the British blockade had begun. Fortune smiled on Bahrain; the ships that Ali destroyed were carrying a very important cargo.

In 410 BC, a Spartan admiral, Mindarus, had suffered a terrible defeat near Cyzicus at the hands of three great Athenian strategists. In one of the most laconic military messages of all time, the surviving Spartan warriors sent the following dispatch back to their HQ. 'Ships lost. Mindarus dead. Men starving. Don't know what to do.' This was one of those moments. Faisal was about to learn that he had just lost three of his key allies in one day – both candidates for governing Bahrain, Mubarak bin Abdullah and Rashid bin Abdullah were dead. Additionally, Bashir, the son of Rahma bin Jabir, had followed his father's example and died fighting a Bahraini fleet, along with all his 150 men. The news was a major setback, and Faisal and Muhammad bin Thani were going to have to revise their strategy. They couldn't get the army to Bahrain; the invasion had been defeated before it had even started.

Meanwhile, Muhammad bin Khalifa's position was improving by leaps and bounds. Two British naval squadrons had taken up positions in Bahrain's defence, one near Muharraq and the other patrolling Qatar's eastern shores. No private shipowner would be willing to transport Faisal's men for fear of losing his vessels. With Qatif's port out of the equation and the invasion thwarted, Faisal was now prepared to consider Ali bin Khalifa's original offer of tribute and arrears. But the situation had changed. Muhammad bin Khalifa and his brother were happy to let Faisal simmer in Doha's summer heat; they were in no hurry to talk. On 20 July, the Wahhabi emir suggested negotiations aboard Ali's *baghla* and sent Ahmad al-Sudairi, chief of al-Hasa, as his representative. As Ahmad's boat drew near and his men called for permission to come aboard, Ali called back: 'If you are agreeable to ask nothing, come aboard, but if you want anything, then don't.' Ultimately, over the course of a few days, Ahmad prevailed on Ali to accept that while Bahrain enjoyed naval superiority, there was no way it could force Faisal's departure from Qatar either. Thus it was that, on 25 July, Ali agreed to pay Faisal 4,000 German crowns in tribute annually and not harass Muhammad bin Thani's people and business, but only on certain conditions. First, Ali insisted on taking up residence in Bida should he choose, and that the few remaining descendants of the late Sheikh Abdullah return to Qais, never again to receive Wahhabi support.

Sheikh Muhammad bin Thani encouraged Faisal to accept the deal. The promise of Bahraini tribute would suggest Qatar was under Faisal's protection. Only Rashid bin Faddal, the chief of Wakra, was unhappy with the talks' outcome and led his people into a voluntary exile in Fars. Once the agreement was signed, the British withdrew their ships and Doha's pearling fleet was, in theory, allowed to get back to what it did best. But in practice Muhammad bin Khalifa was keen to exact revenge on the Al Thani; sending ships to disrupt the pearl harvest, he imposed a crippling economic embargo that wasn't lifted until November 1852. The loss of revenue from two pearling seasons was tough on Muhammad, but he was pleased to have retained his position of authority over Bida, Doha and Fuwairit. He had survived a close encounter to fight another day.

Wahhabi–Bahraini relations remained poor. By 1859, Muhammad bin Khalifa had stopped payment of any tribute and even incited some Qatari tribes to take a much more hostile attitude towards Faisal bin Turki. He, angered by the loss of income, made preparations at Dammam for a second attempt on Bahrain. Britain threatened to sail in support of the Al Khalifa, promising to sink any warship or transport that left the Hasawi coast. Al-Sudairi wrote a letter of complaint to the newly appointed British Resident, Kemball, expressing his belief that both Bahrain and Qatar were Wahhabi client states. 'Know that Bahrain used to give tribute to Emir Faisal and to his father before him for ages past, long before the Sirkar [English East India Company] came to these parts. In like manner the Qatar people are also subjects of bin Saud and used to pay him tribute.'

In truth, Britain's patience with Muhammad bin Khalifa was being sorely tested. The Indian Rebellion of 1857, mysteriously still referred to as a 'mutiny' in various textbooks, had shaken the empire considerably. There were no longer the ready resources to sail to Bahrain's defence each and every time Muhammad bin Khalifa chose not to fulfil his own agreements. Recognising there was nothing to be done against Faisal bin Turki, Britain moved on 31 May 1861 to make Bahrain part of the Trucial system. London recognised the independence of Bahrain and Sheikh Muhammad agreed to 'abstain from all maritime aggressions of every description, from the prosecution of war, piracy and slavery by sea'. Now Britain was responsible for the protection of Bahrain, Faisal's dream of taking the island was over.

Bahrain's new status, however, also meant that the Al Khalifa had no right to use its considerable naval power over Qatar. Muhammad bin Thani was free of Bahraini naval hostility. Though his plan had gone wrong, the outcome was much the same. Muhammad was free of Bahraini harassment and had established himself as the foremost leader in Qatar during a short-lived Wahhabi occupation. Qatar was another step closer to independence. The Al Thani had gained some valuable political experience and Jassim was now in a position to take a much more important role in his father's administration.

6

JASSIM'S ASCENDANCY

JASSIM'S FATHER enjoyed good health throughout his exceptionally long life. Born around 1800, Muhammad kept his experienced grip on day-to-day politics throughout the 1860s. It was clear to most, however, that he had become increasingly dependent on his son. This was a gradual change that had begun a decade earlier, but not one born of a father's faith in his son; there was no sacred concept of primogeniture in the Gulf. Rather, Jassim's ascendancy came through his remarkable strength of character. He had been tried and tested by his forebear with difficult and dangerous tasks from his early twenties, an apprenticeship for power. In 1851, for example, when Faisal bin Turki's army was approaching Doha with unknown intent, Muhammad had sent his 25-year-old son on a secret mission to meet up with Jabir bin Nasir, chief of the pro-Bahraini Naim. Muhammad wanted to ascertain their plans in the face of impending Wahhabi invasion.

This was an extremely delicate matter that might easily have ended badly, for the Naim were no friend to Jassim or his pro-Wahhabi sentiments. Yet into their camp he rode with just a couple of companions and sat with his rivals to talk, returning a couple of days later with their counsel.

Faisal should be permitted entry to Doha, they suggested, as he was too strong to oppose. Barely a week later, Muhammad bin Thani ignored this advice and once more sent out his son, this time with a few hundred men, on a mission to delay the advance of the Wahhabi Emir, Qatar's answer to Fabius Maximus, the Cunctator. Jassim's success, both personal and collective, bought Muhammad the time to draw up plans for a Wahhabi invasion of Bahrain and the installation of a new Al Khalifa leader.

The relationship between Jassim and his father was very close, as we'll see from his poetry shortly. At the political level, however, they could often be diametrically opposed. Towards the end of the 1860s, Muhammad began to favour forming an alliance with the British. Much to Jassim's irritation, he would often write letters expressing friendship to the Political Resident and worry if no reply was received. 'My deputy arrived, but brought no letter from you; I trust the cause of your not writing is good … you have every cause to be pleased with our behaviour.' And when a reply was forthcoming, diplomatic protocol appeared to have blurred into embarrassed patronising, such as in Colonel Lewis Pelly's letter of 1870: 'You are not a British subject but an Arab Chieftain in friendly communication with Her Majesty's Indian Government. Continue to conduct your affairs peacefully and with common sense and you will always find me ready to befriend you.'

The men of Doha would have witnessed Al Thani disharmony most clearly in the extraordinary events of 1871. Four Ottoman flags were brought to Doha from Kuwait. Jassim raised one above his own home, while his father, just 300 yards down the road, chose not to change the flag above his. Father and son would pray in different mosques as soon as the town had two, Muhammad leading prayers at the bigger *jami'* in Bida, while his son prayed in a *masjid* on the outskirts of town. As the historian Frederick Anscombe hints in his book *The Ottoman Gulf*, however, there are signs that Muhammad and Jassim could play a 'good cop, bad cop' routine, in which one might claim he didn't agree with the other, fend off political pressure and maintain harmony within and without Qatar.

The reasons for this discord over policy were well known. Jassim was not at all impressed by the British, though his hostility mellowed with age. It was no accident he had left Bida to go hunting when the British spy Palgrave arrived in 1863. Britain's constant support for Bahrain at that time was a major source of frustration. In any case, he was naturally wary of a Christian nation that had destroyed Qatari towns, imposing its power over a sea that had been the property of none. But the government of India believed Jassim 'mattered' in the region's politics. Thus, a complaining Palgrave was required to fumble his way through the desert and impose his unappreciative company on a Jassim whose Bedouin culture required he receive all guests.

There is a wonderful scene a few years after Palgrave's visit when Jassim's strained-but-loving relationship with his father manifests itself in front of the British political agent Mirza Abed Kasim. Mirza had sailed to Doha in June 1870 to deliver a letter from the Political Resident concerning compensation payments owed Bahrain. Muhammad read the letter and was busy assuring the emissary he would personally resolve the issue to British satisfaction when his son entered. Mirza relates: '[Jassim's] father handed him the Resident's letter; after he read it he said: "Know all of you that this territory belongs to bin Saud, and the prosperity of the people comes from his favour. We will pay nothing to anyone whatsoever." ... I replied I had no business with him, and was addressing the old man, Muhammad bin Thani, and would receive my answer from him only.' You can almost feel the tension as Jassim, no doubt incandescent with rage at Mirza's response, gave salaams to his father and left. Checking that their conversation was again private, Muhammad then told the agent in a low voice: 'Don't worry about him, you have to deal with me, and I will arrange affairs with you,' and Mirza returned to the gunboat *Clyde*.

Perhaps the most obvious of the differences between father and son was the manner of their dress. Unlike his father, Jassim chose to wear the clothes of the Najd. He felt an affinity to the region and its religious values. Throughout his life, Jassim maintained relations with many of its scholars, most famously Sheikh Abdullah Al Shaikh, whom Jassim often consulted. Throughout his life, he would send charitable donations to him for distribution among the region's orphans, widows and poor. He paid for books to be copied and distributed, establishing numerous *awqaf*, religious endowments whose assets were managed by a charitable trust. Despite Muhammad bin Thani's many achievements, the biggest of which was yet to come in 1868, I believe it was Jassim who felt more keenly that attachment to his ancient ancestor, Mi'daad bin Musharraf, one-time governor of the great Jabrin oasis in central Arabia, where you can still find the Mi'daad remembered in place names and charitable trusts as far away as Riyadh.

Post-treaty problems

Not so very long after the ink had dried on the 1861 Perpetual Truce of Peace and Friendship, the Royal Navy shelled Wahhabi fortifications in Dammam. Their intention was to ram home a message that ensured no misinterpretation: Bahrain was under British protection. Faisal bin Turki's son, Abdullah, was also warned to drop any plans he might still harbour for Khalifa subjugation. Though he had lost hope of invading, nonetheless Abdullah maintained that annual tribute should continue, and promptly sought to garner more support from various dissatisfied factions in Bahrain. This was problematic. Britain ruled the waves but was in no position to enforce its rule on land. By February 1862, the new Political Resident, Captain James Felix Jones, despaired of forcing Faisal to drop his claim and urged his son and Muhammad bin Khalifa to negotiate a settlement.

The request fell on deaf ears; relations between all three parties worsened. Faisal even doubled his demand to 8,000 German crowns a year. The British government in India turned to Muhammad bin Thani to head the talks, a role in which he enjoyed little success. As the impasse continued, British frustration with Muhammad bin Khalifa grew, though he seemed blissfully unaware, even poking fun at Abdullah behind the protection of British warships. Contacting the Porte in Istanbul, the Sheikh of Bahrain alluded to the theoretical status of Faisal bin Turki as an Ottoman client, and offered to buy out Wahhabi 'rights' to govern the entire coast from Qatif to Muscat for one million dollars.

Whether or not the Ottomans detected any hint of sarcasm in Muhammad bin Khalifa's absurd request, they welcomed the letter as a means of asserting their own authority in Arabia, a region lost to them two centuries previously. The Turkish governor-general in Baghdad took on the role of mediator, requesting that the British ambassador in Istanbul explain why Her Majesty's navy had bombarded Dammam when they knew it was 'part of the hereditary dominions of the Sultan'. The ambassador's response was blunt.

> Although it may not be denied that, since the Egyptian invasion of Najd in 1840, Amir Faisal has remained tributary to the Turkish authorities of Mecca, his tribute being regarded probably as an offering to the head of the religion, it is certain that the Porte has never exercised any jurisdiction, or attempted to extend its authority over the country …. In point of fact, the Porte has not the power to punish or coerce its tributary; not a single Turkish functionary exists in the country.

It added cheekily that it would be extremely prejudicial to the whole region if that policy were to change.

Endeavouring to keep Ottomans as far from eastern Arabia as possible, the British government in India felt an invigorating sense of urgency to resolve the Saudi–Bahrain dispute. They turned to Captain Herbert Frederick Disbrowe for a solution. To his credit, the officer did research the problem thoroughly and reported that 'non receipt of *zakah*, or religious tithe, for a considerable period is the main source of irritation to the Wahhabi Emir'. With the confidence of a man asked to state the obvious, Disbrowe informed his superiors that should the Sheikh of Bahrain disburse 'his contribution with regularity, Faisal would be willing to come to terms of peace and would cheerfully do his utmost to restrain his subjects and protégés from molesting Shaikh Muhammad bin Khalifa's dependents and from forming combinations inimical to the security of Bahrain'. In short, the tribute had to be paid and Disbrowe would have to collect it. By May 1862, the captain had twisted the necessary arms and packed off 4,000 German crowns to Najd, on the understanding that Faisal would forgo the arrears.

Freed from one problem, Muhammad bin Khalifa gaily involved himself in another. His attentions in April 1863 focused on Qatar's eastern coast. Muhammad sought to provoke a dispute and arranged for the Sheikh of Wakra, Muhammad bin Said Al bu Kuwara, to be brought to Bahrain in chains. Muhammad bin Said was originally a Bahraini vassal but had fled to the Persian coast to escape Muhammad bin Khalifa's employ in 1851. He had returned, after British intercession, eight years later. (Muhammad bin Khalifa also exiled from Wakra a number of others whom he deemed to be 'divers in debt, and disreputable characters used to collect and injure trade or disturb the peace'.) Explaining his decision to imprison Wakra's chief to the British agent at Bahrain, Muhammad claimed his prisoner 'had always some secret correspondence with Emir Faisal and also used to give asylum to everyone who committed any fault or misdemeanour at sea'. The British accepted the explanation, though the agent himself, Hajji Ahmad, observed that Bahrain had virtually decimated the settlement of Wakra. Thus, even though Britain had endorsed Muhammd bin Said's arrest in November 1863, their patience with Muhammad bin Khalifa was now paper thin. It must have seemed to London that the Bahraini protectorate was paying tribute to the Wahhabi state.

Colonel Lewis Pelly, one of the more famous and enduring Political Residents, had initially supported Bahrain's tribute payments in return for peace. The arrangement continued until Faisal was on his deathbed in 1865. But with an expected change of leadership in the Najd, Pelly wanted to make clear that the British protectorate of Bahrain was not subordinate to the Wahhabi state. Unveiling a formula that would maintain payment of tribute but save European face, Pelly decided Bahrain was in fact paying on behalf of its possessions in Qatar and not for itself. This change of interpretation fitted the bill as far as the British were concerned but spelt trouble in the peninsula's east. Bahraini influence had been expunged from the main centres of Bida, Doha and Fuwairit, and was only meaningful among the Naim tribe. Nevertheless, Britain was suggesting that Qatar pay money to Bahrain, which in turn would be passed on to the Najd, even though, as far as Jassim was concerned, Doha already came directly under Wahhabi protection. In one of Sheikh Faisal's last letters, the 80-year old leader insisted that God had given him all the lands of Arabia from 'Kuwait round to Ras al-Hud', necessarily including Bahrain, Qatar and Muscat. The Wahhabi Emir thus laid claim to all of Bahrain and Qatar equally. The Resident dismissed his letter as mere 'pretension'. As the historian Rosemarie Zahlan noted in her book *The Creation of Qatar*, however, the British quietly dropped Pelly's formula when it came up for review in 1880.

The Political Resident had convinced Bombay of his idea by March 1867 and the Governor-General's Council decreed that Bahrain was independent of Abdullah bin Faisal's Wahhabi state and 'owed allegiance to no other power'. Qatar could expect, sooner rather than later, that British ships would call to collect for unrendered, and unrenderable, Bahraini services. Sure enough, the Resident had estimated that since the total annual Wahhabi claim on both Bahrain and Qatar had been 20,000 *krans*, or 4,000 German crowns, Qatar should now pay 9,000 *krans* to Bahrain. Sheikh Muhammad would then pass this amount on to Najd. To make matters worse, Pelly also stipulated that Sheikh Ali bin Khalifa would collect only 5,000 of these *krans*, as the remainder had to be paid to the Khalifa-supporting Naim chief Rashid bin Jabir. Muhammad bin Thani's confidence in the British must have been shaken; he flatly refused to pay Rashid even one *kran*. Was he really being asked to believe that, once tribute was passed into the hands of these two, the money would be amalgamated and transferred to Abdullah bin Faisal in Riyadh?

The proposal was a recipe for disaster, though it didn't come in the form of a Qatari uprising but rather a squabble between the Al Khalifa and the Naim. They argued over the latter's share of the tribute when only 5,000 *krans* had been paid, rather than 9,000. In June 1867, Sheikh Ahmad bin Muhammad Al Khalifa, Bahrain's representative in Qatar since 1863, arrested Ali bin Thamir of the Naim, imprisoning him in Wakra. Sheikh Muhammad bin Thani, who had actually married one his daughters to Sheikh Ahmad, abandoned his tribal loyalties and called on his son-in-law to release the Naim chief in Wakra. But it was Jassim who took control of the situation, escalating the whole affair to the level of an international incident.

As soon as Ali bin Thamir was arrested, his clansmen made for Bida and pleaded with Jassim to free their leader from Khalifa injustice. Honoured that they should come to him, Jassim promised Ali would be freed that very same day, prayed in Doha at noon and was at the gates of Wakra's fort three hours later. Ahmad bin Muhammad had no desire to meet up with his brother-in-law and fled to take ship from Khor Hasan as soon as Al Thani lances glistened on the horizon. Jassim personally broke Ali out of his cell; his prestige in Qatar was at an all-time high. Demonstrating extreme indifference to Al Khalifa sensitivities, he was also aware that Bahrain's treaty with Britain expressly precluded

Sheikh Muhammad from conducting maritime warfare. He was soon to discover how poorly he understood Muhammad bin Khalifa.

Once the Bahraini agent in Wakra had personally informed the sheikh of Bahrain as to events, the sheikh surprised many by publicly expressing his desire for a new, enduring peace with Qatar. In a letter to Muhammad bin Thani, the Bahraini sheikh made a particular point of asking that it be Jassim himself who come to Bahrain to negotiate a permanent peace. With the benefit of hindsight, it seems obvious that Jassim would be either arrested or killed as soon as he turned up in Muharraq, but turn up he did and arrested he was. What conditions must have been like in a Bahraini jail can only be surmised from an inaccurate British report dated 27 November 1867 informing Her Britannic Majesty's Political Resident that Jassim 'has either been murdered, or has committed suicide'.

Prisoner and poet

Born and raised in Ottoman Syria before emigrating to the United States, Maronite Christian and Princeton professor Philip Hitti described in his 1937 book *History of the Arabs* what poetry means to tens of millions of people in the Middle East.

> No people in the world manifest such enthusiastic admiration for literary expression and are so moved by the word, spoken or written, as the Arabs. Modern audiences in Baghdad, Damascus and Cairo can be stirred to the highest degree by the recital of poems, only vaguely comprehended, and by the delivery of orations in the classical tongue, though it be only partially understood. The rhythm, the rhyme, the music, produce on them the effect of what they call 'lawful magic'.

But until you go to a recital of Mutanabbi's poetry in Iraq and have felt the raw emotion of the audience, even Hitti's description may not suffice. I am not about to compare Jassim to the great tenth-century Iraqi poet Abu Tayyib Ahmad ibn al-Husayn al-Mutanabbi, but they both observed the same rules of versification.

In Arabic poetry, rhymed verse falls strictly into one of sixteen different metres, known in Arabic as *buhur*, or seas. It was only in the twentieth century that modern poets regularly dared break with tradition and create their own, unrestricted rhythms. But in Jassim's time, the rules were rigorous and had been for over a thousand years. Every line, or *bayt*, had to use the same measure and end in the same rhyme. Only the talented could express themselves while obeying such strict rules. Thus, like anything worthwhile, the skill of composing poetry could take an age to hone. But time is what Jassim now had, an entire year in fact. Not that he was inspired only in Bahrain; some of his *qasida*s were to come much later on, during his semi-retirement at the beginning of the twentieth century. I'll ask your indulgence, however, as I attempt to translate a few *abyaat* into English verse, and hope that you'll keep in mind that poetry, like a good joke, rarely translates well.

In his life, Jassim composed nine *qasida*s (some claim twelve), each averaging around thirty lines. An authoritative publication of his collected works, his *diwan*, was printed in India in 1910, three years before his death. That they were collected at all highlights their popularity, as poems were rarely written in a mostly illiterate society and might have to go 40 years before being recorded. Poems were generally committed to memory, and so had to be memorable. This was made 'easier' when Jassim chose religious themes that drew on well-known Quranic allusions or references to the Prophetic traditions, known as the Hadith. Jassim varied his style considerably, sometimes writing in a more obvious dialect, other times writing in the High Arabic understood throughout the Arab world. The following six fragments betray a personal and emotional side to Jassim that is seldom seen in history textbooks.

One *qasida*, too long to translate here, describes a love for a beautiful girl a young hero longs to make his bride. Would that we might know her name! Unfortunately, names of countless men and women in Arab history are veiled through the popular use of teknonyms and patronyms, the 'Abu' and 'Bin' of so many historical and contemporary characters.

We have already met one fragment of Jassim's poetry:

> I lifted injustice for no personal gain
>> but to see the weaker freed again.

This might very well refer, in part, to the incident that had brought him to his current predicament. The Naim tribe were to cause the Al Thani grief for many years to come. Indeed, Jassim's son, Abdullah, would still be putting down their rebellions as late as 1937. Nevertheless, when the Naim had begged for his help in freeing their leader in Wakra, Jassim had sworn to effect his release and made good on his promise. He had set aside his own tribal rivalry, and even consideration for Qatar's ties with Bahrain, though the price would be dear. The whole of Doha would have to pay; Jassim's imprisonment was not enough to satisfy Muhammad bin Khalifa, as we shall see. But in the meantime, Jassim had all sorts of concerns, and his poems are very clear.

> How many a servant whom God doth cherish
>> is tried, unjustly in jail to perish
> I see my eyelids tempt a slumber but fail,
>> my sorrows cannot be numbered.

Jassim attached no blame to his father for sending him to Bahrain. In one verse, he describes how his father is like 'the sun's great light that dims the stars' and also heaps praise on his own son, Ali, to whom he gave the nickname Jaw'aan. But not all of his poetry is so romantic in style, and he has no compunction about making clear exactly what he thought of Bahrain and its

British protectorate status. The following two extracts don't beat
about the bush and presumably relate to the British.

> Upon us now idolators, soldiers of disbelief,
>> come with all their scum and guns, misery and grief
> Pagan worshippers, men who misguide,
>> who pray for statues to provide

(By statues, he means the little crosses some Christians keep that
depict a man crucified.) Finally, in this brief taster of Sheikh Jassim's poetry, I'll leave you with his opinion of Muhammad bin
Khalifa, and his company, who had chosen to accept British rather
than Wahhabi or Ottoman protection.

> No judge objects, no scholars ponder,
>> as the kafir flag's pulled high
> Following with love and laughter,
>> their brothers pushed aside

Destroyed but ascendant

While Jassim was in jail, Muhammad bin Khalifa dispatched large
numbers of ships and men, under the command of his brother,
Sheikh Ali bin Khalifa, and Ahmad bin Muhammad, to attack
the people of Wakra, Bida and Doha. This was an action clearly
proscribed in his 1861 treaty with Britain. Nevertheless, the
task force was soon joined by ships from Abu Dhabi under the
command of Zayid bin Khalifa. He had joined the foray so as
to wipe out 'a Wahhabi ally' and a 'popular asylum for fugitives',
meaning the pearl hunters who had fled debt and family to start
anew. Thus it was that in October 1867 the combined forces of
Qatar's eastern and western neighbours sacked Bida and Doha
'with circumstances of peculiar barbarity'. One British official
wrote years later that 'the damage inflicted on the people of Qatar

was estimated at around fifty thousand pounds'. Sheikh Muhammad bin Thani would most certainly have been killed, were it not for Zayid bin Khalifa's men spotting him during the onslaught, extracting from him a promise to pay over one hundred thousand *kran*s (approximately five hundred pounds) and permitting his escape to Wakra.

Muhammad appealed to Abdullah bin Faisal for retribution, but the Wahhabi state was drifting into civil war. Though his brother, Saud, was pushing for control of the Najd and Hasa, Abdullah did take up the Qatari cause, threatening the Al Khalifa 'with hostilities if the booty were not returned, and the inhabitants restored to their homes'. His threat, however, no longer intimidated Bahrain. Disappointed and angry, Muhammad bin Thani and his peers took matters into their own hands and prepared for a retaliatory attack on Bahrain in June 1868. The butcher's bill was high – 60 ships sunk and 1,000 men killed. Neither side could speak of victory, though Bida did succeed in taking a number of Bahraini notables captive. This result saved Jassim's life, since Muhammad bin Khalifa proposed a prisoner exchange and Muhammad bin Thani's son returned home.

With few ships and even less coal, the government in India had been ineffectual at maintaining maritime peace in the Gulf for over twelve months. Their agreements and authority had been flouted publicly. Pelly was determined to restore British order and ordered HMS *Clyde*, *Hugh Rose* and *Sind* to punish all offenders, but most especially Muhammad bin Khalifa. He had already fled to Khor Hasan on Qatar's north coast and applied to the Naim for protection.

By 1 September, Pelly had arrived off Wakra, where the who's who of Qatar came on board to confess their breaches of the maritime truce. All freely admitted their part in attacking Bahrain, but insisted that the looting and destruction of Doha and Bida had required an urgent response. All on board expressed their willingness to sign any document which might secure the general peace and lead to the capture of Muhammad bin Khalifa, who 'during a quarter of a century, was increasingly become the terror of his neighbours'. Five days later, Pelly was at Bahrain demanding the apprehension of Muhammad bin Khalifa, confiscating his ships and extracting reparations for the outrageous events of the previous year. The Resident officially installed Muhammad's brother Ali in the sheikhdom, and promptly imposed on him a fine of 1,000,000 German crowns, one fifth of which was to be paid to Doha in compensation.

The proverb says it is the darkest hour which precedes the dawn. Doha had withstood its darkest year. But now, HMS *Vigilant* dropped anchor off Wakra with a document for Muhammad bin Thani. It began: 'I, Muhammad bin Thani, of Qatar, do hereby solemnly bind myself, in the presence of the Lord, to carry into effect the undermentioned terms agreed upon between me and Lieutenant-Colonel Pelly, Her Britannic Majesty's Political Resident, Persian Gulf'. The introduction alone was an implicit British admission that Qatar was an independent nation led by the Al Thani, and the following five points were all acceptable. It required that Muhammad return from Wakra to his home in Doha; that Qatari ships would not put to sea with hostile intent without consulting the British first; that Qatar would neither aid nor protect Muhammad bin Khalifa, but rather hand him over to the Resident; and lastly that Muhammad was to promote all that would bring peace between Qatar and Bahrain.

And in addition to a seven-gun naval salute for Muhammad bin Thani in front of all the peoples gathered on the shore at Wakra, Pelly issued a second letter to the leading tribal chiefs of the peninsula, informing them of Muhammad bin Thani's recognised status.

> Be it known to all the Shaikhs and others on the Qatar Coast
> that Muhammad bin Thani, of Qatar, is returning with his
> tribe to reside at his town of Doha and has bound himself to
> live peaceably there and not to molest any of his neighbouring

This map by Angelo de Conte Freducci, dated 1555, is orientated with north at the bottom and south at the top. It shows the Arabian Gulf to the left and the Red Sea to the right; the Qatar peninsula can be clearly seen.

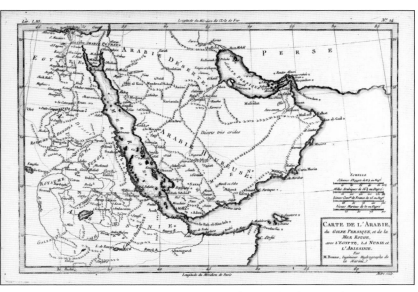

A map drawn some two hundred years later, from *Atlas de Toutes les Parties Connues du Globe Terrestre* by Rigobert Bonne, published in Geneva around 1760. Qatar is again clearly indicated.

Pearl fishing in the Arabian Gulf. This 1870 engraving shows lines attached to the pearl divers, for hauling them back to the surface at the end of the dive.

A group of Bedouin tribesmen, photographed in January 1904 by the German traveller Hermann Burchardt. Burchardt's photographs were the first ever taken of Qatar.

The British Royal Navy inflicted periodic damage on the coastal settlements and fishing and pearling fleets of Qatar in Jassim's time. This photograph shows HMS *Philomel* of the Royal Navy's Persian Gulf Operations Fleet, at anchor in the Gulf around 1900.

A fishing boat hauled up for repair on the seashore at Doha in the 1950s. The building in the background, part of what is known as the Diwan al Amiri, was constructed for the Emir and is still used for government business today.

Fishermen tending their nets on the seashore at Al Khor, a fishing village in eastern Qatar, in the 1970s.

A traditional pearling vessel, seen here in 1985, proudly flies the Qatari national flag.

Bedouin camelriders in the Qatari desert. This photograph was taken in the 1970s, but the riders' skills are the same as in Jassim's time a hundred years before.

Bedouin tribesmen of the 1950s making coffee and tea.

A traditional meeting of dignitaries and tribal leaders in Qatar in the late 1970s.

A rugged stretch of coastline near Fuwairit, Jassim's birthplace in north-eastern Qatar, photographed in the 1970s.

The fort at Wajba, scene of Jassim's decisive victory in 1893 over the Ottoman forces under Mehmed Hafiz Pasha. This photograph was taken around 1930.

The coastal village of Lusail, near to Bida and present-day Doha, was Jassim's summer retreat. He discreetly ruled from Lusail in his later years, and was buried there after his death on 17 July 1913.

The coastal settlement of Wakra as it appeared in the early 1980s.

Traditional mosque in Doha,
photographed in the 1950s.

Sand dunes to the
west of Wukair,
photographed in the
1970s.

The stunning architectural spectacle of the present-day corniche at Doha, capital of Qatar (above), is no less impressive when lit up at night (below).

A far cry from the small fishing settlements of Jassim's time, the modern port of Ras Laffan in north-eastern Qatar is a major export hub for petroleum and gas products. The port was completed in 1996 by Qatar Petroleum and covers 56 square kilometres.

The Pearl Monument on the corniche in Doha is a proud acknowledgement of Qatar's heritage, and of the pearls that provided a livelihood for coastal communities in Jassim's time.

tribes. It is therefore expected that all the shaikhs and tribes of Qatar should not molest him or his tribesmen. If anyone is found acting otherwise, or in any way breaking the peace at sea, he will be treated in the same manner as Shaikh Muhammad bin Khalifa of Bahrain has been.

At nearly seventy years of age, Sheikh Muhammad bin Thani was finally recognised by the Gulf's predominant power as ruler of Qatar for the first time. Pelly said little to explain his motives for drawing up the agreement, but Bahrain's Political Agent in 1905, Captain Francis Beville Prideaux, explained the status of Qatar under this agreement decades later.

> At some time between 1851 and 1866, Sheikh Muhammad bin Thani was enabled to consolidate for himself – no doubt with the good offices of the Wahhabis, to whom Sheikh Muhammad of Bahrain had made himself so very objectionable – a compact little dominion containing the towns of Wakra, Doha and Bida, the independence of which from Bahrain was practically established and ratified by the Government of India in 1868, when a formal agreement was first taken from Sheikh Muhammad bin Thani.

His explanation clearly indicates that Britain viewed Qatar as an independent state with the Al Thani at its head, a landmark agreement in Qatar's history.

The following year, just as the pearling season was about to begin, Muhammad's deputy, Khamis bin Juma Al bu Kuwara, arrived at the British residency in Bushire to arrange the payments stipulated in the 1868 agreement. Qatar was still to pay 9,000 *krans*, equivalent to about forty pounds, of which 4,000 would be paid to Rashid bin Jabir, chief of the Naim tribe, and 5,000 to the chief of Bahrain for ultimate payment to the Wahhabi government. This Naim payment was still tough for Muhammad to bear, and led to one of the few occasions on which he lost his temper in front of a foreign representative. Visiting him in Doha, Major Sidney Smith observed how Muhammad 'got greatly excited' and flatly refused to pay Rashid bin Jabir anything, saying: 'I have employed others to protect me, and have paid them four thousand krans and more, why should I pay the Naim anything, who have done nothing?'

In a letter to Muhammad, Pelly explained why:

> It is understood that this payment of tribute does not affect the independence of Qatar in relation to Bahrain. But is to be considered as a fixed contribution by Qatar towards a total sum payable by Bahrain and Qatar combined, in view to securing their frontiers from molestation by the Naim and Wahhabi Bedouins, more particularly during the pearl diving season, when the tribes of Qatar and Bahrain occupied at sea, leave their homesteads comparatively unprotected.

Thus the payment of tribute by Qatar was intended to ensure the security of a newly emerging independent state, and was not a tribute paid by a client state to its suzerain.

Within a few years, the stipulation of payment to the Naim was being ignored and was officially removed in 1880. More than five decades later, the unknown British civil servant who had actually calculated how much Qatar should pay, its 9,000 *krans*, had his sums revealed in a book published in Delhi in 1933. It appears he arbitrarily assessed Muhammad bin Thani as good for 2,500 *krans*, with the Mahandah, Al bu Aynain, Naim, Al bu Kuwara, Keleb, Sudan and Amamara paying the rest in amounts varying between 500 and 1,700 *krans*.

Jassim soon took effective steps to establish tribal harmony round much of the peninsula, though Khor Hasan was mostly beyond his reach, along with much of the north-west. But even this situation was resolving itself in Qatar's favour. Muhammad bin Khalifa had begun to plot against his brother Ali from his exile in Kuwait and then Qatif. Ali was dead by 1870. Bahrain

had a three-month interregnum before Isa bin Ali was installed
at Pelly's insistence. As Bahraini power faded, some Qatari tribesmen were enticed to leave the west coast and settle in Wakra,
a development noted by Captain Sidney Smith when he came
to Qatar in April 1869 on a review of the post-treaty situation
in Qatar. Smith also noted that British Indian subjects who had
come to settle in Wakra were prospering. Pelly was also pleased
that Muhammad did not enter a dispute without first referring to
the British agent at Bushire. Thus when the Bahrain half of the
Al bin Ali began helping themselves to vessels from the Qatari
pearling fleet, the Sheikh of Qatar referred the whole matter to
Pelly, as he felt it his responsibility 'as the independent ruler of
Qatar' to inform the Resident 'before anything has taken place
because you understand matters'. Pelly appreciated Muhammad's
cooperation, particularly when he opposed Abdullah bin Faisal's
plan to send troops to Oman. But Jassim was not so pleased with
the way things were developing, and his time had arrived. By
1870, Muhammad bin Thani was over seventy, effective power
rested solely in the hands of Jassim, and he wanted British influence removed.

7

OTTOMAN QATAR

NAPOLEON once described Europe as a molehill; all the world's greatest military leaders, he felt, had made their reputations in the East. This was why he really took 40,000 soldiers to Egypt in 1798 (an invasion originally considered by Louis XIV more than a century earlier). The three-year occupation of Alexandria and Cairo was nothing to do with 'menacing British trade' or 'bringing scientific enlightenment', as is so often claimed. Sadly, Napoleon was disappointed with both cities, and this disdain rubbed off on his men, who grew increasingly indifferent to the local sensibilities. Some troops would convert mosques into cafés, others would fly tricolours from minarets. The French military police chief, Barthelemy, was said to feel cheated if he hadn't lopped off daily at least half a dozen rebellious heads. But there was a uniquely positive feature of the invasion too, and that was its large contingent of civilian administrators, scientists and engineers. Two of them concern us: Jacques-Marie Le Père and Mathieu de Lesseps.

Le Père was there to build roads and bridges, but his wide range of civil engineering interests led him to investigate ancient attempts at constructing canals between the Mediterranean and the Red Sea. The military implications of linking the two would not have been lost on Napoleon. The 35-year-old Jacques-Marie was packed off to excavate Necho II's canal works between the River Nile and the Suez Gulf. Unfortunately his surveying skills let him down on this occasion, and he reported to Le Petit Caporal that such a canal was impossible since the difference in water levels was as much as nine metres. Nevertheless, his work fascinated a fellow colleague, Mathieu de Lesseps, who would become the French consul-general in Alexandria after Napoleon withdrew and Paris re-established diplomatic relations with Egypt in 1803.

While there, Mathieu would also make friends with a promising young Ottoman army officer called Muhammad Ali, whom he recommended for promotion in a letter to the Sublime Porte before returning to France in 1804. The following year, he probably choked on his morning coffee as he read that Muhammad Ali was now Muhammad Ali Pasha of Egypt, after leading a successful palace coup. Their friendship would prove most fortunate. In the meantime, Mathieu told the young sons he bounced on his knee of Egyptian adventures and the Canal of the Pharaohs. Mathieu de Lesseps must have told enthralling stories, for half a century later his son Ferdinand travelled to Egypt intent on building the Suez Canal.

Ferdinand was fortunate that Said Pasha, Muhammad Ali's fourth son, not only knew of him and his father, but could speak French fluently. In fact, Said had been educated in Paris, and his Francophile inclinations were partly responsible for Britain attempting to delay the whole Suez project. Nevertheless, 30,000 slave labourers began work on 25 April 1859 and a similar number kept working every day for another ten years. On 17 November 1869, the first person to enter the lockless canal was the French Empress Eugénie in the imperial yacht, followed swiftly by England's Peninsula and Oriental Navigation Steam Ship *Delta*, of the same P&O company bought by Dubai well over a century later in 2006. For the first twelve months of operations, it seemed as if the Suez project would fail. But the initial trickle of ships soon turned into an almighty torrent and the Arabian peninsula was suddenly a few thousand miles closer than it had ever been.

The Suez Canal promised all sorts of trade benefits for the Ottoman Empire too, though the Porte was concerned about an increase in European shipping in the Red Sea. Istanbul had good reason to fear this development. It had failed to put down the Greek revolt and proved itself hard pressed to fend off Austria. France had begun to prise Algeria from its grasp after 1830. The Turkish government would have to redouble its efforts in order to prevent a similar fate for its eastern provinces, but early indications didn't bode well. The Royal Navy had helped lay a telegraphic cable linking India to the southern tip of Ottoman Iraq in the 1860s, with scant explanation. The suspicion, of course, was that the cable was meant to go all the way to London. And while land was being lost in the west, Britain seemed to be making a pile of money in the Ottoman east. The Lynch Company, for example, enjoyed a virtual monopoly on all steamer traffic on the Tigris and Euphrates, and had done for 30 years, despite repeated attempts to set up a rival service. Baghdad's disquiet was almost palpable between 1867 and 1872. Some very rich British entrepreneurs were openly discussing plans to invest in a rail line between the Mediterranean and the Gulf – as if the project had nothing to do with the government that actually controlled the land. The train service was never realised, but the talk of it helped convince the Porte that London was intent on forging a land link from Egypt to India.

The year 1869, therefore, was received more as a portent of doom than of opportunity. The loss of Mecca and Medina in the Hijaz was unconscionable. The response was an expedition into western Arabia and Yemen in 1870. It went well; northern Yemen fell quickly (or at least the towns did). The shell that blasted through the capital's city gates brought instant surrender. (The hole it made was never repaired and can still be seen at Bab al-Yemen to this day.) Military success, and relative inexpense, encouraged Istanbul to continue the campaign. Their timing was impeccable; it was the perfect moment to establish authority in eastern Arabia too. In 1870, the Second Wahhabi State was on the verge of collapse. An intense rivalry between Abdullah and his brother, Saud, had weakened the whole structure which their father, Faisal, had so carefully built up. Control of eastern Arabia would also support Turkish authority in Yemen, since it would end the use of Najd as a hinterland that could offer refuge to tribes beyond the lengthening arm of Ottoman law. Istanbul would also benefit from direct land links between Iraq and the Hijaz when it came to collecting *zakah* and escorting pilgrims on the haj. The capture of Hasa would permit troops to neutralise any Wahhabi threat to Iraq. Finally, the conquest of the eastern seaboard would help secure the shipping lanes between Basra and Jidda. Iraqi farmers were transporting ever more wheat to the Red Sea port after contracts were signed in 1864. The trade had to be protected from attack; controlling Qatif, Hasa and Qatar would allow for this protection.

Ever since the Russian tsar Nicholas I supposedly described the Ottoman Empire as the 'sick man of Europe', European governments were certain its collapse was imminent. The knowledge that Islam's last caliph was exiled in 1924 – ironically seven years after Nicholas II was executed – has also led many a historian to see Turkish failure in all its nineteenth-century undertakings. This is a mistake. As its soldiers demonstrated at Gallipoli in 1916, the Ottoman army was no joke. And Istanbul still had very capable leaders. The Sublime Porte was fortunate to have one of its best in Baghdad. Midhat Pasha was ready, willing and able to execute the invasion of Najd and the eastern coast of Arabia by the end of 1870. His expedition would give significant strategic depth to Ottoman Iraq.

Midhat was exceptional. His long career first saw him as a governor of the Ottoman provinces of Bulgaria, Danube and Syria. On return to central government, he was appointed chief director of confidential reports and second secretary of the Grand Council, a reward for his honesty. He twice served as Grand Vizier, the second most important position in the whole empire. He had a natural talent for rooting out corruption, and was always thorough in his planning. Unfortunately for the empire, his abilities provoked jealousy among the very people who should have supported him. He was often given every rotten task going, though more often than not he would succeed at it anyway. Nevertheless, his rivals managed to have him banished from Istanbul by 1876. Tellingly, though, and for most of his career, whenever he submitted his resignation, it was refused. Later on in his life, he was caught up in the intrigues of the Young Ottomans reform movement, and left Turkey for London, studying the methods of a government he was so often attempting to thwart. Midhat's loyalty to the state was, rather insultingly, questioned in the last three years of his life. Escaping a hastily passed down death sentence for treason, and settling at Taif in Arabia, he was probably assassinated in 1884. (Turkey eventually brought his body back to Istanbul for burial 80 years later.) But in 1870, when his interest in Jassim bin Muhammad began, Midhat Pasha was governor of Baghdad, planning the invasion of eastern Arabia.

Ottoman invasion

The gossip in Doha in October 1870 was different from the usual 'can you believe what he did' variety. Something quite out of the ordinary had captured the public imagination. The steamship *Asur* had docked and a couple of strangers of Turkish appearance had disembarked. The captain of the ship introduced them as traders, though they showed no interest in buying or selling anything. In fact, they were spies, probably the worst-ever spies in history. The duo could only have been more obvious if they'd stuck false moustaches on top of their bushy Ottoman moustaches. The pair had been sent by Midhat to get a feel for the land. Their idea of a pleasant conversation was not one about the pearl harvest that year, or the high price of rice. These spies were special and would ask questions more along the lines of: 'What would you think if the Ottoman army marched into town?' No doubt the agents did their best, but on their return to Baghdad, Midhat Pasha probably felt something was not quite right and sent the following note to his general, Nafiz Pasha. 'Instead of heading straight for Qatar, it would be more advisable to contact the people of Qatar yourself and give them guarantees. By winning over the former Bahrain sheikhs as well, persuade the Qatari people to appeal to the [Ottoman] State before going there.'

Midhat Pasha wanted to delay the occupation of Qatar until 1871; he needed to move against Najd first. The long-running dynastic rivalry provided the perfect opportunity to fulfil all the objectives of his detailed plan. Abdullah bin Faisal had been pushed out of power by Saud in 1869, and Midhat had sought him out, through the offices of the Kuwaiti Sheikh Abdullah bin Sabah, to offer his assistance and subdue Najd. Abdullah was pleased to accept the help, though he proved a most unreliable ally. The governor of Baghdad could now move decisively, for he had already obtained authority from the Grand Vizier Ali Pasha for the campaign in June of that year. General Nafiz mobilised and Abdullah bin Sabah accompanied him and his 300 vessels, glad to accept Ottoman suzerainty over Wahhabi intimidation. Nafiz made quick work of defeating Saud's forces. Hasa province, including Qatif and Uqair, were under Ottoman authority before winter had begun. The only fly in the ointment was the inability to continue to the Najd, and its capital Riyadh, but that was achieved the following year by proxy through Muhammad bin Rashid of Jabal Shammar. Only Qatar remained; and Midhat was hoping for a swift intervention as Wahhabi remnants were using the peninsula's south as a base from which to take potshots at the Ottoman army.

In a report written in December 1871, Midhat Pasha claimed

an invitation to invade was sent by Jassim and his father. Both had apparently 'reiterated the necessity of despatching troops to Qatar'. The details in Midhat's reports suggest Jassim had done just that, though his father's role is less certain. 'The rebels who have taken up arms are backed up by Bahrain which supplies them with food and ammunition. As the distance between Qatar and Bahrain is negligible, goods shipped from there are easily shipped to the coast of Qatar.' The clearest evidence that Jassim was supplying important information to the Ottomans was that Midhat knew the names of the 'troublemakers' from the tribes of Ajman and Murra who would most likely resist.

Jassim's father would remain quite vague about his role in the following years, but in the meantime Sheikh Abdullah bin Sabah arrived at Bida before any Turkish soldier had set foot in Qatar. He had with him four Ottoman flags. Jassim took one and hoisted it above his own house immediately. The second flag was given to his father, Sheikh Muhammad, who later claimed he had not taken it, preferring to keep his own red one. (It ended up in Wakra.) The third was presented to Ali bin Abd ul-Aziz, a leading figure at al-Khor, a town north of Bida. The last flag was sent to Khor al-Udaid, on the border with Abu Dhabi. Ottoman rule in eastern Qatar was established by cloth rather than lead.

In no time at all the flag-raising frenzy attracted the Royal Navy gunboat *Hugh Rose*, which anchored off Bida on 19 July. Major Sidney Smith, the Assistant Political Resident, was most unpleasantly surprised. No report of Ottoman troop movements had reached him. Going ashore, he decided to ask Muhammad bin Thani, rather than his son, for some short, sharp facts as to what was going on. He had chosen the wrong Al Thani. Muhammad may have been old, but he was a seasoned diplomat who knew how to avoid awkward questions. The sheikh began by explaining how he was personally unhappy about the situation and had hoped for a treaty of protection similar to Bahrain's. Specifically, he told the major: 'Colonel Pelly placed me here and made me what I am, while I live I will do what seems right to him.' Smith probably tried to tell the veteran leader that Pelly was going to be apoplectic, but Muhammad continued. The Ottoman flag had been hoisted at Bida, he informed the young officer, on the orders of the Ottoman commander at al-Hasa, and not his orders, of course. It was just that Nafiz Pasha was not a man to be refused. Smith's temples were probably beginning to throb. He knew that there was not a single Ottoman official in town. Muhammad continued, considering aloud how technically, and traditionally, 'the Ottomans had supremacy on the land of Qatar'. Smith was wondering by now whether this was geriatric contradiction or plain old mockery. Muhammad was certainly weaving a rich tapestry of fact and fiction. He had just one more weft to add. The word was that Sulaiman bin Zahar, the chief of Basra, was of the opinion that the Ottomans would bring all the land between Basra and Muscat under their jurisdiction and that any chief desiring the Ottoman flag would receive it, together with Ottoman protection. By the time the venerable sheikh had finished, I'm sure Smith would have reached for whatever they took for headaches in 1871, certainly not the yet-to-be-marketed aspirin.

Reading between the lines, Muhammad bin Thani was probably informing the British that Qatar would no longer pay 9,000 *krans* to Bahrain. But whatever Muhammad's exact position, Smith felt Jassim and his father had hoisted the Ottoman flag willingly and told the British consul-general in Baghdad the same. Colonel Herbert sent a brief letter to a gloating Midhat. 'The Ottoman authorities with the expedition have acted contrary to Your Excellency's intentions and repeated assurances.' Midhat didn't reply – he didn't need to. Jassim's acceptance of the flag was based on his own pragmatic considerations and not achieved by force of arms. Kuwait had accepted Ottoman sovereignty in exactly the same way. Midhat could only wish all military conquest was so simple.

British outrage is hard to understand. Jassim had changed his allegiance to the Porte for several excellent reasons. Before the Saudi civil war, Jassim had always been a sincere ally to Abdullah bin Faisal, who had continued to aid Jassim right up until 1870. In that year, for example, remnants of Abdullah's confederates continued to harass some clans of Naim to such an extent that many looked to leave for Bahrain. One Naim notable, Abdullah bin Muhammad, even told Major Smith that Jassim's use of Wahhabi loyalists had turned life for the Naim into a living hell. 'We have been turned out ... our chief, Rashid bin Jubbur [sic], is inland and afraid to show ... under the circumstances, if we proceed to Bahrain, who will answer for our wives, children and property?' But Abdullah was losing the fight against his brother. The tribes of Najd didn't want him. Jassim needed a new ally at the very same time as the Ottomans were interested in returning to eastern Arabia.

In the meantime, Qatar was increasingly vulnerable to raids by Saud bin Faisal's troops. The year 1871 was a particularly bad one; Saud's supporters had cut off Doha's water supply. Even if Jassim had chosen an alliance with the British, their ships could never have stopped Saud's attacks. But Ottoman troops were newly arrived in Hasa, and could put up a defence. Similarly, Britain had shown itself unwilling, and probably unable, to prevent Al Khalifa money from reaching the Naim in north-west Qatar. Naim loyalty to Bahrain spelt the end of Jassim's bid to unite the peninsula. The Ottomans, on the other hand, could put troops on the ground, and probably in places like Zubara, where they would really help the Al Thani cause. At a personal level, Jassim's memories of his Bahraini cell, the terrible sea battle of 1868 and Doha's recent destruction would naturally have left him inimical to Bahrain's protectors, the British. The alliance with Midhat meant Jassim might play one empire off against another, and so benefit his vision for Qatar. The new situation sometimes left Jassim in a precarious and vulnerable position, but his tenacity ultimately brought rewards to the Al Thani and the peninsula during the 1870s.

The Ottoman arrival

In December 1871, the Ottoman authorities at Hasa finally sent a detachment of 100 troops and a field gun to Bida, under the command of Major Omer Bey. Once again, this was solicited in an invitation from Jassim, who now took over completely all his father's responsibilities. The 1868 agreement with the British, which had made Muhammad bin Thani a *primus inter pares*, was now obsolete. Jassim would claim that it had always been obsolete, for it had had no teeth. The British weren't willing to commit troops; they hadn't landed an army in the Gulf for over fifty years. The Al Thani cause could not be progressed by ship, it needed armed men and cavalry. Jassim was convinced the Ottoman military could be manipulated into stopping any encroachment by the tribes of north-west Qatar, and possibly even end Bahraini interference once and for all.

Welcoming the Ottomans into Qatar, however, and helping them extend their control from Basra up to the eastern limit of the peninsula, was fraught with risk too. Jassim would have to expect some changes and challenges to his authority, and Midhat Pasha didn't disappoint. The governor had plans, drawn up long before the invasion of eastern Arabia. The Baghdad governor combined the four *kaza*, or districts, of Hasa, Qatif, Qatar and Najd into a single organisational structure called the Najd Mutasarrifiyya, or governorate. 'Once the campaign is over,' he instructed his administrators,

> the title of Qayamaqam [or district head] of Abdullah bin Faisal will be transformed into Mutasarrif [provincial governor]. Abdullah shall appoint Qayamaqams to Qatif, Qatar – and to smaller places, administrators. However, it should be seen to

that if such appointments are likely to cause unrest among the Arabs, they must be put off until later. Furthermore, canonical judges from the Hanbali sect shall be appointed to Qatif, Hasa, and Qatar and, if possible, to Riyadh and Qasim … the canonical obligation of collecting *zakah* may take place but no other measure is to be imposed.

These changes were mildly irritating for Jassim. For starters, his new Qayamaqam title came with no salary. Samuel Goldwyn's witticism that 'a verbal contract isn't worth the paper it's on' is most à propos. He resented the fact that the Ottoman representative in town was also Doha's new judge. Worse, it now seemed Qatar would actually be paying more in *zakah* to the Ottoman state that it had been paying Bahrain.

Nevertheless, the change was fairly smooth and had not affected his standing among the tribes. Within a couple of years, it must have seemed that Midhat wanted to run Qatar as Britain ran Bahrain. So long as peace and trade were maintained, and occasional visits tolerated, internal affairs could be left to the locals. Jassim's official appointment as Qayamaqam, instead of Omer Bey (despite some objection in Baghdad), had enhanced his status and prestige. The Ottoman stay was quite short and painless too. Most soldiers were withdrawn by the autumn of 1874. Jassim revelled in having a protector who gave him such a free hand to rule. He could also use his position to avoid negotiations when they were not in his interest. In the winter of that year, some Bahraini ships had bombarded the west coast and landed tribesmen in Qatar to pursue and kill men of the Banu Hajir in a bloody six-hour attack. Jassim wanted to extract revenge but received word that Bahrain had dispatched a peace delegation. In fact, Sheikh Isa had sent his own brother, Ahmad, to smooth over relations. A few years earlier, Jassim would have had to receive the delegation. But that was then. Ahmad got an imperious rebuke rather than a reception. The State Archives of Qatar record Jassim's remarks, as he refused Ahmad permission to disembark. 'Qatar and the places subordinated to it being Ottoman territory and myself an official representative of the Ottoman State, you should know better than to come to me.' The ship returned to Bahrain. Sheikh Isa would be under no allusions as to Jassim's intention. He was going to attempt to extinguish Bahrain's influence in Qatar.

Before I describe how this was achieved, you may be wondering what Britain was up to, especially as the Porte claimed Bahrain as part of their empire too. But it is the very complexity of Anglo-Ottoman relations which explains Jassim's initial success. Naturally, the British government never officially accepted the Porte's claim of sovereignty in Qatar. At the same time, however, it also avoided exacerbating tensions or provoking diplomatic incidents lest it upset a very delicate relationship. This was because British policy, even before the Crimean War, was to maintain the territorial integrity of the Ottoman Empire, and so preserve the balance of power in Europe. For British policy-makers in London, Qatar was a 'vexed question' that should not be allowed to end in conflict. It was for this reason that London and Delhi seldom saw eye to eye on Qatari issues. The British government in India had a quite different perspective. It needed to keep the Gulf as British as possible for all sorts of reasons: to limit French ambitions in Iran, provide a link in the route to India, and maintain access to Iraq and its great rivers. The result was a policy of deliberate vagueness. British diplomatic consensus was to accept the reality of the situation, but not publicly acknowledge it. Thus, London never gave any legitimacy to the Ottoman position on Qatar, but obviously acknowledged it by steering clear of confrontation. Midhat was well acquainted with the policy, and chose to deal with British Bahrain in exactly the same way.

Some historians, like Zahlan, doubt that Jassim was aware of the many aspects of Anglo-Ottoman relations. This may be true, but by the same token many British and Ottoman officials in the Gulf were equally ignorant, and did not appreciate the game Jassim was playing. With genuine courage and strength of character, he intuitively knew how to neutralise their power. Many who have tried to walk the political tightrope between two opposing powers have fallen into an abyss; history is full of such examples – from Alcibiades to Quisling. But not Jassim; he crossed to the other side and emerged in a far more powerful position than the one he had inherited from Muhammad. In 1874, he needed to establish his authority over the north-west and push back Al Khalifa claims for good. He recognised that the town of Zubara was absolutely key to his plan. By welcoming any excuse to promote conflict there, and exacerbating the polarisation of tribal loyalties, Jassim felt confident he could draw the British and Ottomans into a confrontation neither wished to end in a fight. He would manipulate ensuing negotiations to have the British do his job for him. He would use the British to keep the Al Khalifa out of Qatar.

The struggle for Zubara

Zubara's status was hotly disputed. Bahrain and Britain could both respond swiftly to the least provocation, which Jassim regularly provided through raids and misinformation. For example, on 16 August 1873, Major Charles Grant informed a new Political Resident, Colonel Edward Charles Ross, that a detachment of some one hundred men had embarked from Qatif to accompany the Ottoman officer Husain Effendi to Zubara. In point of fact, Grant had misinformed Ross, but the effect was the same. The Bahraini chief Sheikh Isa bin Ali reacted angrily and told Grant that something had to be done. The Naim clans living near Zubara were 'his subjects under treaty', as the retired Colonel Pelly would bear witness. Grant had no way of knowing the truth of the Bahraini chief's claim, but suspected it was improbable. He observed that Bahrain hadn't maintained power in Zubara for years, and Al Khalifa authority was weak 'if it existed at all'.

Sheikh Isa couldn't afford to let the issue go; he feared the intrigues of Nasir bin Mubarak, a rebel Al Khalifa clansman who claimed the right to rule Bahrain. Isa had good reason to be nervous; he had come to power in 1869 when his father Ali had been killed in battle against the combined forces of his own brother Muhammad and Nasir bin Mubarak, grandson of Abdullah bin Ahmad. His plan was to re-establish, once again, a garrison at the town for the explicit purpose of hunting out Nasir. Ross was as keen as anyone to help the Naim, since they had never accepted Ottoman suzerainty, but he realised too that Isa's claim to Zubara, even if were valid, could not be endorsed or enforced by Britain. Ross told Grant on 28 August 1873 that Isa 'had not the power if he wished to protect tribes' in Qatar and ordered the major not to intervene on the peninsula on his behalf as 'his so called rights, were involved in uncertainty'. Grant also offered Sheikh Isa some fairly frank advice: 'Remain strictly neutral and keep aloof from all complication on the mainland with the Turks, Wahabis, etc.' But the advice fell on deaf ears. Isa would try to persuade the British of his rights to Zubara over the next six months. His persistence irritated the government in Delhi, which ordered Ross to demand that Sheikh Isa give up any hope of possessing Zubara. 'It is desirable that the Chief should, as far as practicable, abstain from interfering in complication on the mainland' of Qatar. Unlike Jassim, the government of India was keen not to give the Ottomans any excuse to station troops in Zubara, which would do little for maritime peace in the region.

By 1874, Isa was of the opinion he would have to take matters into his own hands, and perhaps attack Zubara without British approval. His change of attitude followed news that Nasir bin Mubarak had taken up positions on the Qatar coast. It seemed clear Jassim was encouraging him to deal with the Naim tribesmen who might still support the Al Khalifa. And should Nasir be successful and re-establish the fort at Zubara, he might try to instigate a rebellion inside Bahrain itself. By the summer, Sheikh Isa's concerns were more acute. Before he had an opportunity to sneak money and supplies to the Naim, Nasir and a force of Banu Hajir tribesmen had gathered at Zubara in a bid to infiltrate Bahrain. On this occasion, the British ships of the Bombay Marine had prevented an attack, but there was little to celebrate. On returning to Zubara, Nasir had taken out his frustration on any Naim tribesmen who came to hand. Though Nasir didn't enjoy much fortune in the larger skirmishes, with no support from Bahrain and Jassim blocking supplies from the south, it was only a matter of time before Al Khalifa influence over the Naim would end.

Sheikh Isa's six-hour attack on the Banu Hajir of Qatar did little to stem Jassim's push into the north-west. In fact it did the opposite. For once Ross got wind of events, he forbade Isa from carrying out anything similar ever again and was of a mind to punish him. On 10 December 1874, Ross told Isa in no uncertain terms that Bahrain had no possessions in Qatar whatsoever. He also made it clear to Isa that he should keep well away from the 'feuds on the mainland'. From now on, Bahrain was just an island. Any hint of objection, Ross added, and the British would withdraw their ships and protection. Isa wrote a few letters in one last attempt to change some minds, but to no avail. By May 1875, Jassim had his victory. Isa had to accept he could not support the Naim. A Qatari nation was one step nearer. This was an extraordinary accomplishment. If you had spoken to Jassim's father just ten years earlier, he probably wouldn't have considered Zubara as part of Al Thani territory, even though his own father, Thani, had lived there for a time. But through careful manipulation of two empires, and the consequent clashes he had instigated, Jassim was well on the way to winning sovereignty over the whole of Qatar.

Three years later, in 1878, Jassim and Nasir bin Mubarak led 2,000 men to the north, ostensibly to deal with reported acts of piracy. Jassim took the opportunity to sack and destroy Zubara. He had subdued the remaining Khalifa remnants of the Naim. What was more, the Royal Navy had prevented Bahrain from rescuing his supporters after the attack. He needn't have bothered, for Jassim sent them to Bahrain himself, along with any Naim tribesmen who wished to leave. Zubara as a town ceased to exist. Its fort was destroyed. All that remained was its strategic importance. The only news that lessened Jassim's joy over his many successes that year was of his father's passing away. It also meant, however, that Jassim was no longer a prince regent; he was now the Sheikh of Qatar. The Ottoman government sent Zayyid Pasha, Mutasarrif of Najd, to Bida to congratulate him on his new position and assure him of Istanbul's support for the future; he then asked for 10,000 *krans* in tax to be paid to the Porte!

In many ways, 1878 had proved an *annus mirabilis*, but Jassim's success in dealing with his external enemies was about to be challenged by internal division. In November 1879, the Al bu Kuwara tribe moved from Bida back to Fuwairit, denouncing Jassim's pro-Ottoman policy. In 1880, the Banu Hajir of Hasa captured a boat belonging to Wakra and made a series of raids on Doha. In 1881, the Banu Hajir were joined by some of the remaining Naim. Perhaps the most embarrassing event, however, came later that year. The Ajman stole and drove 450 camels out of Qatar. Jassim appealed for Ottoman help in their recovery, but they made no effort to assist. It seemed that the Ottomans were only a fair-weather friend. After ten years of Jassim flying the Ottoman flag, the relationship was about to take a turn for the worse.

8

QATAR'S UNITY TESTED

IN DECEMBER 2010, a US marine poking around a few dark caves in southern Helmand province, near the Pashtun town of Marja, came across something quite out of the ordinary. He could just make out its long, thin shape, half hidden among rocks, though it was carefully wrapped in a blanket. A few seconds later, he was looking at an ancient rifle – probably hidden from British patrols more than a century earlier. It was a Martini–Henry rifle, the best thing money could buy for the rank and file back in the 1870s and 1880s. Its robust, self-cocking, lever-operated, single-shot action embodied the weapon of empire. The rifle's action had been designed in 1870 by the Swiss national Friedrich von Martini, while its seven-groove rifling was patented by a Scotsman, Alexander Henry. Around a million were made and used throughout the world's colonies for over thirty years. They didn't fire the familiar .303 round, but .450s. Some versions even fired .577s. Within a few years, the firearm was in action against Zulus, Boers and Russians.

Not to be bettered by the British, the Ottomans had turned to an American manufacturing company in Providence and ordered thousands of Martini–Henry replicas for their troops in south-east Europe. The Turkish General Staff were most pleased with the result, but their men, outnumbered by Russian forces five to one, still lost Romania, Bulgaria and Montenegro by 1878. Nor were all Turkish soldiers issued with the rifle, certainly not the troops stationed in Qatar during the 1880s. And here was the ultimate irony. Jassim, who had never frowned on a healthy arms smuggling trade between Bahrain and Qatar, had managed to acquire and supply his tribesmen with the latest rifle on the market. Many of the Al Thani were better armed than the Ottoman troops sent to guard Doha!

The weapons' arrival could not have been more timely. By 1882, the Qayamaqam was facing various internal problems, even challenges to his authority from confederates. The Al bu Kuwara, for example, were deeply dissatisfied at pledging allegiance to any Ottoman and moved out of Doha, which was attacked several times by the Manasir and Awamir tribes. In 1884, the threat of imminent attack by the Ajman tribe was so great that no one dared go to the pearl fisheries that season. In a bid to deal with the dissent, Jassim first sought to tone down hostilities with his external enemies, particularly Bahrain. He even visited Sheikh Isa's brother in eastern Qatar when he had brought his hawks and hounds on a hunting expedition.

Jassim now planned a campaign, confident the prestige and plunder it generated would reunite all dissenters. He decided upon seizing Khor al-Udaid, situated on his border with Abu Dhabi and part of the Trucial coast. He hoped to restore the hundreds of camels stolen a year earlier and demonstrate to his fellow tribesmen that befriending the Turkish military had its advantages. He also expected the 400 Ottoman lira he was paying in tribute annually would buy some significant support. He was mistaken.

The Ottomans were only too aware that Khor al-Udaid, technically under their protection, was claimed by Abu Dhabi. Any attack would ultimately draw in the British. For this very reason, there was no way they would willingly involve themselves, despite giving verbal assurances to the contrary. Jassim left

Bida expecting to meet up with an imperial battalion. They never showed up and Jassim was forced to withdraw. This was to be the first of many occasions when he failed to receive backing. The Al Thani must have felt Qatar's suzerain was in far greater need of them for maintaining the Ottoman claims in eastern Arabia than vice versa. It was Jassim's strength which held Qatar together; the Mutasarrif stationed only a few dozen men in the whole peninsula.

And even if the Porte was not willing to join Jassim in campaign, it was inexcusable that they didn't protect him from the imposition of British 'justice'. The government of India had special leverage in Doha and Wakra in the early 1880s, thanks to their Hindu Indian subjects, the Banyans. In the Gujarati language, *banyan* means merchant, and not a species of tree such as Daniel Defoe had Robinson Crusoe build his home in. The Portuguese picked up the word to refer specifically to Hindu merchants and passed it along to the English in the seventeenth century. By 1634, English writers began to tell of the banyan tree, a tree under which these merchants would conduct their business. It provided a majestic, arboreal shade for merchant markets and meetings, and gradually came to mean the tree itself. Banyans first came to Qatar, settling in Wakra, during the rule of Jassim's father, Muhammad. Numbers grew quickly when they found their niche as the middlemen who sold pearls in Bombay. That was all well and good until the first signs of a trade dispute, when Banyans called on the British Political Resident, rather than accepting Arab or Ottoman justice. Jassim would feel frustrated when he, the Qayamaqam of Qatar and its foremost tribal leader, was bullied into paying fines and accepting British judgements passed on him for alleged infractions committed on Ottoman and Qatari soil.

The government of India would also send to the region travelling consuls who had followed special courses in private learning establishments, the East Indian Schools – a proto-'British

Council'. Often these men were accompanied by officers dressed in the garb of Muslims. Their mission was to influence and suggest that prosperity and protection could be secured only by British subjects. In our times, and since the 9/11 attacks, it is fascinating how the British Council has reduced its budget in Europe so as to expand operations in 'high priority' regions, such as Iraq and Afghanistan, to 'steer Muslims away from extremism'. Plenty of people are critical of the change. Charles Arnold-Baker, author of *The Companion to British History*, put it best. 'The only people who are going to read our books in Beirut or Baghdad are converts already.' Jassim must have found the presence of such 'missionaries' disturbing, but there was little to be done unless the Wali of Baghdad was prepared to take up the issue.

Despairing of Ottoman intervention, Jassim took matters into his own hands and closed all Banyan shops in 1882, expelling the community from Doha. Once again, this brought an instant response from the Political Resident, who sailed to Doha in the misnamed HMS *Arab* and not only forced the Qayamaqam to pay compensation of 8,000 rupees, which was taken from Jassim's own funds, but insisted Qatar take back a people the British were using as fifth columnists. The historical record has plenty of reports which show that Banyans, based in Qatar, passed on the local news, views and gossip to British officials. Smaller ships would also visit the pearling fleets during the summer, as historian Zekeriya Kursun puts it, 'to win the hearts and minds of the local people and induce them to receive documents proving their loyalty to Britain'.

It wasn't until 1884, when the corvette *Merih* arrived at Doha to investigate Jassim's claims, that the Mutasarrif of Najd began to grasp the situation. Ottoman political inaction had permitted Britain to become a judicial institution in Doha. It was not only undermining local respect for Ottoman authority, it was making it impossible for Jassim to maintain his public support. Any misunderstanding that may have remained was removed with Jassim's letter of resignation. He no longer wished to be Qayamaqam. His letter claimed it was because 'he had made the intention to go on Hajj'. The governor of Baghdad, however, could read between the lines. Passing the resignation on to Istanbul, he informed the Porte that much of the blame fell on the Mutasarrif of Najd. And just in case Istanbul was considering accepting the resignation, an accompanying note made clear there was next to no one who could possibly fill Jassim's sandals. The possible exception, Ali bin Jassim, had already rejected the offer with disdain as soon as the Mutasarrif had suggested it. The point was conceded, and Baghdad removed the Mutasarrif, appointing Nezih Bey as his replacement. Istanbul clearly felt it better to dismiss the officials who had failed Jassim and embarrassed the empire.

In the meantime, Jassim needed his freedom to tackle the many challenges that were coming thick and fast from friends and enemies alike. He persisted in his request to resign throughout 1885, though assured the new Mutasarrif he was still a loyal Ottoman subject. He offered his son Khalifa as Qayamaqam, and promised to accept any other choice popular with his people.

> Should either of these alternatives prove not to be acceptable to your side, then, please appoint a Qayamaqam who is an Arab or Turkish. If you disagree with me, I hereby declare that I will have to leave Qatar for good, and go somewhere else, whether Bahrain, Oman, Iran or elsewhere. Having served the Ottoman State and taken care of Qatar's protection for the last fifteen years, I am begging now to be excused from my office.

On the face of it, Jassim's threat seems an empty one. How could the Sheikh of Qatar leave Qatar? His instant allegiance to the Ottomans, however, coupled with their continued absence – except when it was time to collect *zakah* – had cost him political capital among his people. There were many men who would happily seek to exploit the deteriorating situation for their own benefit. Some tribesmen would claim independence; others would promote themselves as Qayamaqam candidates to the Ottoman administration. One man, Muhammad Abd ul-Wahhab, did both. He was the son of a wazir of Bahrain whose sister was the widow of Jassim's father. He had become sheikh of a small village called al-Ghariya and was a keen observer of the political scene. Sensing that Taqi'l-Din Pasha, the governor of Baghdad, might finally and grudgingly accept Jassim's resignation, Muhammad decided to be the 1886 thorn in Jassim's side.

Muhammad Abd ul-Wahhab

A year earlier, around two hundred people of the Al bu Ghaz passed through Wakra on their way to Fuwairit. These migrants dominated Ottoman correspondence for the next two years. They would claim independence, protest harassment at the hands of Jassim's men and even considered applying for British sponsorship. The peninsula was teetering on the brink of collapse. Jassim's most dangerous opponent had once been a friend. Muhammad Abd ul-Wahhab had big ambitions and would one day become a salaried member of Qatar's Administrative Council. Jassim initially dismissed Muhammad's political machinations as a mild irritation, but tensions grew and soon an Ottoman corvette was permanently stationed to keep an eye on developments. The reports it sent back presented a chaotic situation at the ordered Ottoman administration. Many of these reports adopted Muhammad's point of view; he was far more prolific in his correspondence than Jassim. Essentially, the dispute boiled down to the following: 'The Qayamaqam of Qatar with his gang have attacked the village of al-Ghariya, and killed seven men of Muhammad's and stolen a great amount of cash and property.' (Al-Ghariya was a village between Bida and Fuwairit.)

The Ottoman judge in Doha, Al-Sayyid Muhammad Amin, was asked for his opinion of the affair, but he suffered a good deal from virtual isolation in Doha and was mostly ignored by the local population. He had little grasp of the facts. Amin did, however, report a rumour: al-Ghariya had prepared a report for the British consul at Bushire, appealing for his protection. Ottoman hackles were further raised on an additional rumour that the British vice-consul to Muscat had sailed to Qatar for a private interview with Jassim.

> The talk with Jassim lasted for a couple of hours. The exact account of their talk remains a mystery. However, according to Jassim, he was asked what had been his gain in serving the Ottoman State. The topic of Jassim's conflict with Sheikh Zayid of Abu Dhabi was also on the agenda, and perhaps also the likelihood of an imminent entering of Fuwairit under British protection and of a great exodus from the region.

The judge had touched a raw Ottoman nerve. By the end of 1885, the Turks saw a British stratagem behind every mishap, usually unjustly. Ali Riza, the Wali of Basra, needed no more evidence than the hearsay of a lonely judge and informed his superiors that 2,000 Qataris 'were about to apply to become naturalised British subjects'. Ottoman support, what little Jassim enjoyed, was based on the understanding the sheikh could control Qatar. If sections of the peninsula escaped his authority, then it was time to back new leadership. The Mutasarrif in Najd, specifically sent to aid Jassim, secretly planned to have him replaced, hoping to kill two birds with one stone. Muhammad Abd ul-Wahhab could stop the 2,000 becoming British and become the new Qayamaqam.

Muhammad had proved himself an eager ally and given every indication to Nezih Bey he could rule the town independently of the Al Thani and garner tribal allegiances quickly. In December 1885, Muhammad felt confident enough to suggest Nezih urge that the tribes switch their allegiance to him. 'You must write letters threatening prominent persons like Banu Tehrim, Murra, Banu Shaif, Banu Hajir and Manasir.' (Curiously, the letter suggests that Muhammad had also been in contact with the British.

'Tell them not to attack the non-Muslim communities of the state [the Banyan] ... they all come for shopping at frequent intervals to Hasa.') Lastly, Muhammad washed enough dirty linen to convince Nezih that Jassim had to go. He related how Jassim's relative Ali bin Rashid – a local tough guy – had been collecting un-Ottoman but traditionally Bedouin taxes on the Qayam-aqam's behalf, alleging that it was an absurd tax of 80,000 rupees on the Al bu Ghaz in Wakra which had driven them to Fuwairit in the first place. Muhammad pointedly asked whether any of this money had ever filled Ottoman coffers. Jassim's rival was very confident of success by 1886, openly calling for his appointment as Qayamaqam and openly acting the part, visiting Sheikh Isa of Bahrain and attempting to win over tribes affiliated to the Al Thani. He was pushing his luck.

Jassim had a habit of retiring to the desert with kith and kin each year to sojourn there for a few weeks at the end of each January. In 1886, he appeared to be following his normal prac-tice, but perhaps with a few more tribesmen than usual. Within a week, he had launched a surprise attack on Fuwairit. The raid was not designed to capture the well-populated town of his child-hood, but was extensive enough to make clear who was in charge. The next day, Jassim attacked al-Ghariya even more successfully, evicting his uncle-in-law back to Bahrain. Muhammad swiftly wrote to Nezih with the details, and called on him to intervene. Nezih had no one to talk to, however. Jassim had returned to the desert, rejoined his family and finished off his holiday, reappearing only to hand the Mutasarrif yet another letter of resignation on 25 February. This time he decried not only the lack of Ottoman support, but the tolerance shown to the Qayamaqam's detrac-tors. Nezih was delighted to receive the resignation and strongly endorsed it, arguing that Sheikh Jassim had been troubling both the Mutasarrif and the Supreme Council at Istanbul with his occasional threats of abandoning the empire. He even called on Baghdad to appoint his recommendation for a new Qayamaqam since a 'country without a government looks like a house without an owner'.

Confident Baghdad would back him, Nezih had not grasped the reason for his appointment. He had been sent to support Jassim and strengthen the credibility of Ottoman authority among Qataris and those who interfered in Ottoman affairs. He had achieved little in this regard, however, involving himself in tribal conflicts and, worse, backing one side against another. Perhaps, too, he had only half understood the vicissitudes of tribal struggle in which Monday's enemy could be Tuesday's ally. Meanwhile, Muhammad still attempted to court tribal support, specifically from the Banu Hajir of Salim bin Shaif, who had joined in the attack on Fuwairit. He was an experienced chieftain, and accepted Muhammad's gifts but offered nothing in return. Back at Bida, Jassim denounced Muhammad as an agent of British-backed Bahrain, a man who would have delivered Fuwairit to the British and fought against Qatar. Muhammad was exposed as a chieftain without a tribe. The recklessness of the Mutasarrif's decision to accept Jassim's resignation must have begun to dawn. Nezih had nobody to take Jassim's place and had demonstrated to everyone in Doha an Ottoman inability to control events on the ground; rather events controlled him.

Inevitably, the Sublime Porte once more declined to support any proposal which meant Jassim might be replaced. Istanbul was only too aware such an action would dissuade every local leader from Udaid to Muscat from submitting to Ottoman authority. Accordingly, on 3 March 1886, the Supreme Council instructed the Wali of Basra that Jassim must remain the Qayamaqam – he was a key balancing factor against the British, the man who had established a predominant position in the Gulf through his remarkable strength and political appreciation of the 'bigger picture'. Nezih Bey had to accept the decision and a lesson in tribal affairs: leave it to Jassim. Only a tribesman knew how to play politics in a tribal society. As if to prove the point,

Muhammad Abd ul-Wahhab instantly reconciled his differences. Jassim even wrote to state his pleasure at renewing an old friendship and called on Nezih to reward the man he had fought against just a month earlier. Muhammad was given a salaried appointment at Darain in Qatif (and outside Qatar!). Jassim had won the challenge, but no thanks to the local Ottoman administration. It was only the Porte's appreciation of Jassim's worth which had prevented a most unfortunate turn of events. But for all its wisdom, Istanbul still proved incapable of appointing officials in eastern Arabia who appreciated the local situation.

Tithes, titles and trouble

Nezih didn't last much longer in his position as Mutasarrif of Najd, but his replacement — from Jassim's perspective — was to prove equally annoying. The empire was squeezing as much money out of the provinces as it could to pay the huge amount of interest on its loans from Britain and France. Qatar was not to escape this revenue-raising initiative. The new Mutasarrif was determined to establish a customs house at Bida. But Jassim had become experienced in breaking in new officials, and decided the best way to frustrate the Ottoman plan was to reduce Bida's importance. He decided to withdraw to a place in the desert called Ras al-Zaayen, declaring that he had severed his links with the capital and was no longer responsible for the running of the country. From now on, anything to do with Qatar's administration, as Jassim put it, should 'first be referred to God and then to the Turkish Government'.

Jassim's tactical retreat had created a security breakdown at the pearl market in Bida by July 1887. The Turkish gendarmes were wary of using force, afraid of upsetting tribal sensibilities by arresting the 'wrong' person. It was only a matter of time before defenceless Hindu Banyans began to be victimised, as they were accused of monopolising the pearl trade. Two were seriously wounded in an incident guaranteed to attract some Royal Naval interference.

Jassim's brother, Ahmad bin Muhammad, and his son Khalifa, moved to protect the Indian community but it was too late. Since the British didn't recognise Ottoman authority over Qatar, they decreed that Jassim was the party responsible for the attack on British subjects in Bida. The new Mutasarrif in Najd, Akif Pasha, was conspicuous by his absence. Only the Basra telegraph station reported that British pirate ships had appeared off the coast of Qatar. But Jassim's plan to bring the provincial governor to heel was about to backfire. With the help of the Sheikh of Bahrain, Edward Charles Ross, the Resident in the Gulf, confiscated pearls worth 20,000 Indian rupees belonging to Jassim. Worse, all the British Indian residents at Bida were removed to Bahrain and the Assistant Resident himself arrived for a patronising attempt at reminding Jassim of his responsibilities. Though he sent an emissary to Bahrain to negotiate, and the case was eventually settled by the payment of around six thousand rupees as compensation to the injured British subjects, Jassim was furious. Local Ottoman officials were silent once more. They collected tax but gave no protection.

Jassim had to restore order in Bida himself and was obliged to return, determined to make the Mutasarrif and his superiors understand the damage done not only to him, as the Qayamaqam, but to Ottoman prestige in the region. In a letter dated 3 November 1887, Jassim wrote to insist any plaintiff who lived and worked in Qatar should henceforth come under Ottoman jurisdiction. The missive could almost be sarcastic, were it not for the harsh financial consequences of Turkish unwillingness to involve themselves in issues relating to British meddling.

> The British feel restless in the face of my loyalty and every now and then they display their animosity ... such are the injustices to which I am subjected because I am an Ottoman citizen and protected by the Ottoman state ... I should like to suggest that, with a view to having my rights protected, the plaintiffs should henceforth have recourse to Ottoman courts of justice and act according to the judgements that are to be pronounced therein.

The letter was passed from official to official until it reached the Ministry of the Interior in Istanbul a month later. An official response came in December.

> The cruel treatment of Shaikh Jassim is due to the Shaikh's loyalty and affection for the Ottoman State and to the unrewarded excellent services he has rendered as Qayamaqam of Qatar ever since the capture of Najd. Shaikh Jassim is being deterred from serving the Ottoman State by harsh treatments in order that he may pledge allegiance to the British. This is unbearable. Jassim is an Ottoman citizen and a government official. All disputes should be settled by Ottoman courts of justice. Even in grievances related to cases of default, the courts dispensing justice should be the aforementioned ones. Under the circumstances, resort every now and then to cruelties and extortions from British officials instead of referring the cases to the appropriate authorities is not compatible, nor is it reconciled with international laws and treaties.

Jassim had won his political point, though it had taken almost six years for the Ottoman administration to act.

The Wali of Basra, Mehmed Hafiz Pasha, recommended the measures needed to protect Ottoman interest in the peninsula, and prepared to visit Jassim personally. Before leaving Iraq, however, he requested two things from his superiors. First, he urged the Porte to protest about British meddling in Qatar's judicial affairs to their ambassador in Istanbul. Secondly, on 12 January 1888, he proposed to the Grand Vizier that Jassim should be awarded a new honour, which might give a lift to proceedings as he attempted to improve relations. Mehmed suggested the title of Kapucibasi (Head of the Palace Gatekeepers) for Jassim's faithful services and loyalty to the Ottoman Empire. And so it was that on 29 February 1888, Sultan Abd ul-Hamid II issued a decree confirming the award that was so prestigious among the Ottoman aristocracy. Mehmed arrived in Bida at the beginning of March to confer the new honour.

It is amazing the variety of titles that have been offered by kings, emperors and sultans over the centuries. Very often honours had started off life meaningfully, but that all began to change in the seventeenth century. Louis XIV of France, for example, loved turkeys and kept them in a special enclosure near the canal at Versailles, bestowing an important noble with the dubious title 'Captain of the Royal Turkeys'. Kapucibasis had at least begun life with a serious job. They controlled access to the Ottoman Sultan and thus the one or two who existed in the fifteenth century actually had a position of authority. The Kapucibasi kept his power right up until the rule of Mehmed II (died 1481), who appointed only one. After him, however, title inflation began in earnest and the position came to mean very little. By Jassim's time, there were literally hundreds of ceremonial palace gatekeepers. A pragmatic, self-confident tribal leader, Jassim was not impressed. He didn't need titles. He needed the Ottomans to show some backbone in the face of British interference.

Recovering from the obvious disappointment, the Wali was astounded at the scale of local Ottoman incompetence and sent many recommendations to the Grand Vizier on his return to Basra a week later. Mehmed proposed the permanent deployment of an Ottoman vessel off the coast of Qatar and upgrading the garrison at the old fortress of Bida to accommodate one infantry battalion of 250 men. The official added he was of the firm opinion that British confiscation of Jassim's property was indeed part of a campaign of repeated attempts at breaking Jassim's loyalty to the state. Finally, Mehmed touched on the status of Zubara, suggesting it be settled again and generate revenue for the Ottoman treasury. He was confident Jassim could induce the Naim, among others, to settle there.

The Mutasarrif of Najd, Akif Pasha, made his own recommendations for change that might support Mehmed's plans. To date, there were only two Ottoman institutions in Doha, the courthouse and a small garrison of gendarmes. Akif proposed a deputy Qayamaqam, a secretary and assistant secretary in addition to an administrative council. Since almost all residents of Qatar were poor, the members of the council from the local population were to be paid a monthly salary and so take the council's duties seriously. A harbourmaster for Doha, who would collect fees from native boats and monitor foreign ships and passengers, was named (but never assumed his post). Akif furthermore wished the state to erect buildings in town and levy taxes on pearl dealers and other merchants. Finally, to complete Qatar's defence against British intrigue, the Ottoman army would deploy at Zubara and Udaid.

None of these proposals would be acceptable to Jassim, who only wanted the Turks to help him extend Qatar's borders and turn up in Bida when it mattered: when the British attempted to force their will on him.

Personal loss and revenge

Inside Qatar, Jassim's situation had improved dramatically; his tribal authority was restored and the Ottomans seemed at last prepared to deal with the British. But during the last few years of the 1880s, he had been engaged in a low-intensity conflict in the south-east. The point at issue was the allegiance of a colony of Banu Yas tribesmen who had left Abu Dhabi and settled in Khor al-Udaid. This was their third term of exile – they had come to Udaid for brief periods in 1835 and 1849 – and on each occasion it had caused friction between the rulers of their original and adopted homes. Sheikh Zayid complained that their presence in Udaid threatened the prosperity of his people, while Sheikh Jassim welcomed it as a convenient means of extending his authority over the area. The poor old Banu Yas claimed to be independent of everyone, but kept a Trucial and Ottoman flag ready at all times, just to be safe. They further complicated the situation by partaking in occasional acts of piracy on both their neighbours. The long and the short of it was that every other year had seen Qatari or Abu Dhabi tribesmen raid each other. In many ways the conflict endured because Zayid was a true Bedouin who had fought some fairly fierce opposition in his youth, even killing Sheikh Khalid bin Sultan of Sharjah in single combat. He owned his own pearling fleet and was protective of his lands. In any other context, they might well have been friends, but as neighbours there could only be trouble.

A raid by Abu Dhabi confederates in 1888 had particularly grievous consequences. Some two hundred and fifty tribesmen had attacked Bida and killed the few dozen men they had found there, including Jassim's most beloved son, Ali. Jassim came to describe the incident in a letter a few weeks later.

> We never thought that they would dare to this extent, nay even a great power would not have dared to act thus against a town under the protection of the High Government. We were all away from town, and my son Ali and some other inhabitants only were in the town. They attacked them about the time of Fajr prayer [just before dawn] on the eighteenth day of Ramadan and all were taken unawares. They set up an uproar, and whoever came out of his house in response to the call was slain in front of the door of his house, and God so decreed that Ali my son was among those who were slain, and an equal number or perhaps more, wounded ... by the time I had arrived, the whole thing was over.

Sheikh Zayid attempted to negotiate a settlement, but was told only the deliverance of his dearest son for immediate death would suffice. In May 1888, Sheikh Jassim applied for Ottoman support to inflict a grievous retribution, but he clearly didn't expect to receive it, writing: 'the Government is neglectful ... I do not know whether this neglect emanates from herself or that the high officials do not report these matters to the Government in the correct manner'. But their support hardly mattered any more. Jassim, and his three sons Khalifa, Abdullah and Abd ul-Rahman, were determined to fight and called on the many friendships and alliances Jassim had built up over 40 years in power. Many powerful leaders responded to the call, including Abd ul-Rahman bin Faisal and Ibn Sabhan of the Rashid, the two most powerful tribes of the Najd. Their combined forces reached as far as Liwa in Dhafra in Abu Dhabi by January 1889, brandishing their Martini-Henri rifles.

I would like to write, as some historians have done, that Jassim merely destroyed date plantations. The truth is, however, that, blinded by grief, Jassim inflicted a vicious revenge. The British Resident in Bahrain described an account that had reached him a few weeks later of the attack on the nearby fort of Dhafra.

> The fort is only an enclosure, made of bricks, and about six to seven feet high, and it contained two citadels without parapets and loop-holes; they were all crying out loudly, and begging Jassim to grant them safety of their lives, but they heard them not. They then told them to evacuate the fort under Jassim's protection. Some of them came out of the fort and they fired a volley on them and charged them. About twelve men of Jassim's party were slain, and some men were wounded. They then carried away slaves and other booty.

Other villages suffered a similar fate. Jassim himself put the number killed at al-Jowa at 520. The desert may have soaked up more blood than we can possibly imagine over the millennia, but this was a bad day by any standards.

Jassim now returned to Bida, expecting a counter-attack within weeks. He prepared the town's defences and pressed men into a force of about eight hundred, expecting Zayid capable of raising between four and five thousand. Though outnumbered, Jassim hoped the disciplined Turkish troops might make up for lack of numbers. Typically, the Ottoman officers were determined to play as small a role as possible and refused to operate under any circumstances more than four hours' march from town. But the attack never really came, just a series of skirmishes and counter-raids by forces of both sides. This continued until the Al Thani penetrated into Sila, east of Khor al-Udaid, by boat in August 1889. His men had to be recalled; however, when the Resident, Ross, warned Jassim that Sila belonged to Abu Dhabi and was under British protection, Jassim consented to withdrawal, but maintained that Sila was within Qatar and 'therefore within my territory'.

Returning to Bida, he learnt that the Turks, far from looking to back him up over Sila, were intent only on implementing their proposed administrative reforms. In June 1889, a memorandum was sent to the newly appointed Wali of Basra, Hedayet Pasha, who was asked for permission to appoint 'to Zubara, west of Qatar, an able administrator conversant with the region ... under whose command there shall be some forty or fifty cavalrymen and infantry gendarmes'. Hedayet perceived only the economic benefits of the project and happily agreed, but failed to appreciate that garrisoning Zubara would bring him into direct conflict with Bahrain and Britain. Hedayet wrote back:

> By our Sultan's grace again, two villages will be formed in no time in Zubara and Udaid thanks to which commercial affairs and the pearl trade will thrive both at the said places and in Qatar. Thus, it will be possible in the future to realise an annual revenue of two thousand and five hundred liras derived from the *ihtisap* tax [market tax] like that which exists in Qatar and Ujair.

The Wali of Basra believed the changes were intended to bolster the Ottoman treasury, reviving the pearl trade from Zubara to Khor al-Udaid. He seemed only vaguely aware that this reform might appear to others as an attempt to strengthen Ottoman positions along the Gulf coast and prevent encroachment by foreign powers such as Britain. Jassim was pleased to discover that the Ottoman Council of Ministers approved the expansion plans in

December 1889, authorising the immediate settlement of the two towns at the extreme ends of Qatar. But Jassim was never going to permit the rest of the proposed reforms. Any attempt to impose them would be prevented, even by force if necessary.

9

THE OTTOMAN DEMISE

T HERE ARE TWO TYPES of pirate in this world. First, you have the beard–lighting vandal whose idea of living is to hit people with anything handy, grab all valuables in sight and bury them for some unfathomable reason. He is the Hollywood pirate who enjoys bellowing the hearty songs which start 'Yo, ho, ho' and reading – probably with a torch under his bedsheets – as many John Masefield poems as he can stomach. But back in the real world, piracy had never been a genuine lifestyle choice. It is little wonder over the centuries that a few buccaneers were rescued from execution by supportive crowds. Working all hours on a cramped, half-starved ship, only to remain in continual debt, was enough incentive to make any seaman think twice. The words of one young British sailor, William Scott, echo into this new age of Somali piracy. Just before William was hanged in Charleston, South Carolina, he shouted: 'What I did was to keep me from perishing. I was forced to go a–pirating to live.' The thousands accused of the crime in the Arabian Gulf of the nineteenth century were very much of the second category.

Jassim never frowned on the smuggling that was rife around Qatar's shores for a very good reason – he knew the desperate poverty that drove it. Occasionally he benefited from such 'pirates', particularly when arms were involved. One American historian suggests Jassim even organised the running of guns himself. Whatever the truth, the Ottomans certainly gave him a lot of freedom to control his own affairs. On the few occasions they successfully managed to intercept a shipment, Jassim warned the Mutasarrif based in Hasa that his people would inevitably turn to foreign smugglers if the weapons were not returned for their own defence. As it happens, the weapons weren't returned, but the Ottomans understood the limits of Turkish power. They were restricted to Doha and as much sea as their one patrol boat could cover. No Qatari felt the Turks' supreme authority in their day-to-day lives and nothing could be accomplished by a few officials and their modest garrison without the agreement of Jassim. And this was the way Jassim wanted things to stay.

The Sublime Porte had a very different point of view. It was keen to promote the administrative reforms that would necessarily enhance Ottoman power, and planned to garrison more troops outside of Bida. Everyone from the Wali of Baghdad, down through the Mutasarrif of Najd to the *mudir* at Bida was all too aware they had never extracted significant tax revenue. To change this meant challenging Jassim's authority. He had let them into Qatar, but he hadn't given them power. Jassim wanted Ottoman muscle in the face of British meddling and help in defending the state's borders from Bahrain and Abu Dhabi, but not a genuine occupation with all its colonial baggage. He conceived of the Ottomans as he had the Second Saudi State, whereby he would pay *zakah* and call on Faisal bin Turki's support when threatened, but not let Faisal's men settle for good. Jassim liked the freedom he had come to enjoy over the last twenty years and would have rejoiced on hearing that the British did not want more Ottoman troops in Qatar either.

On 9 December 1890, the British ambassador in Istanbul had

made the following query to the Ottoman government: 'Her Majesty's Embassy has the honour to request the Sublime Porte be good enough to inform it as to the truth of a report which has reached Her Majesty's Government to the effect that the Imperial Ottoman Government intend to establish posts at Zubara and [Khor al-] Udaid on the Qatar Coast.' The Porte ignored the request for information, but the Foreign Office was not about to drop the issue. Three months later, London wrote again, insisting it could not acquiesce in the occupation of either Zubara or Khor al-Udaid. Ambassador White in Istanbul laid out his government's position to Said Pasha, the Ottoman foreign minister, a few weeks later. His weak argument ran that since Abu Dhabi claimed Khor al-Udaid and had signed a maritime peace treaty almost forty years earlier, the town also enjoyed British protection. (White failed to mention, however, that Qatar had not been a signatory to this treaty.) On 4 July, Istanbul responded, stating both towns were part of the Wilayet of Basra and had long been administered by the Qayamaqam of Qatar. They also, correctly, pointed out that the Anglo-Abu Dhabi Maritime Agreement of 1853 had no bearing on the situation whatsoever. The argument went back and forth for months, but the Ottoman response was always the same: the Porte had a legal right to establish administrative posts in both towns, and that the Wali of Baghdad would thank the political agent in the Gulf not to contact Arabian chiefs on any matter without prior permission.

While the two empires squabbled, Bahrain accused Jassim of encouraging his son-in-law, Nasir bin Mubarak, to prepare a force at Zubara for dethroning Sheikh Isa. This was highly implausible, but whether true or not, the Ottomans had an additional reason to garrison Zubara. The Porte argued it was as keen as London that the maritime peace not be disturbed. By mid-August, the Ottoman Council of Ministers decided to implement the reform programme drawn up three years earlier and sent a battalion of soldiers to the region under the command of the Wali of Basra,

Mehmed Hafiz Pasha. Imposing an Ottoman administration that could collect tax and control Qatari villages, however, was not something Jassim was ever going to accept. He once again tendered his resignation as Qayamaqam, stopped paying tax to the Porte and waited for events to unfold.

The Battle of Wajba

Mehmed had arrived in Najd by October at the head of the 11th Marksmen Battalion, comprised of around two hundred soldiers. He mustered a further 100 mounted gendarmes and 40 Ukail cavalrymen before the battalion set out for Bida in February the following year. He had even brought a small cannon to complete the image of military strength with which he hoped to intimidate Jassim. Mehmed was going to demand payment of taxes owed and force Jassim to accept the proposed Ottoman reforms that would weaken his grip over Qatar. But Jassim had no intention of negotiating on Ottoman terms, and camped at Wajba, about twelve miles west of Bida, ignoring repeated demands to present himself. The ex-Qayamaqam had determined Mehmed would have to come to him if he wished to talk. Jassim's repeated refusals to show up at Bida also gave him time to assemble thousands of men from the Al Thani, the Manasir and the Banu Hajir. Some four hundred men from other Qatari tribes also joined the sheikh. Armed with their Martini-Henrys, these men posed a well-armed, highly mobile force well acquainted with the terrain and perfectly adapted to their environment.

The sandy depression that is Wajba was a rare oasis in the Qatari interior. In Jassim's time, there were three masonry wells providing good water, and a walled garden. Until quite recently, the place had changed very little – it was just a large fort and a ruined summer house full of raised tiled baths surrounded by mosaics. The brick wells have survived the ravages of time, though they are now disused. On the whole, it seems a thoroughly unremarkable place, yet it was from here, on 26 March 1893, that Jassim's men would set out to fight the Turks.

A few days earlier, Mehmed Pasha had sent an ultimatum, urging the sheikh to present himself at Bida and pledge loyalty to the Ottoman state. Unmoved, Jassim sent one of his relatives, Sheikh Khalid, with a bold response. Unless Mehmed was willing to withdraw his troops from Qatari soil, the Sheikh of Qatar would be disinclined to enter into negotiation over the 10,000 Turkish lira in taxes claimed. Neither man could afford to lose face now. It was clear to all the time for talk had ended; rather it was time to find out who really controlled the peninsula. Jassim made the first move, sending a sizeable detachment of horsemen to Salwa with orders to cut off Bida's communications with provincial headquarters at Hasa. This was achieved successfully and quickly, and the detachment remained on patrol in the south to intercept frequent Ottoman attempts to call on the support of tribal reserves. As a consequence, Mehmed was unable to contact the clans he had paid for support, under the command of Sheikh Mubarak Al Sabah of Kuwait.

The Wali retaliated by arresting Jassim's younger brother, Sheikh Ahmad, and over a dozen other Qatari families, imprisoning these hostages on board the warship *Merrikh*, accusing them of spying on Ottoman troop numbers for the benefit of their fellow tribesmen at Wajba. Jassim immediately offered to pay the 10,000 Turkish lira in return for their release, but to no avail. Major Yusuf Effendi led out Mehmed's troops, cavalry and cannon, intent on destroying Jassim's positions at Wajba and all the men he found there. After two hours, the Ottoman troops had passed the fortress of Shebaka, and were just half an hour's march from Wajba. It was here that they came under heavy gunfire from some three to four thousand of Sheikh Jassim's hastily formed infantry. Taken unawares, the Ottomans fell back immediately to regroup near Mesaimeer, where the 11th Marksmen put up much more of a fight, killing around four hundred Qatari warriors. But the Turks were still forced back to Bida, harried all the way by Qatari cavalry. Over half the Turkish battalion lay dead, and a further 55 were wounded. They had lost their colours, cannon and over a hundred and fifty rifles. Jassim's victory was near, but he still needed to take the fort at Bida, where the remnants of a once proud force now cowered.

Deserting his soldiers in town, Mehmed fled to his ship and brought the corvette's guns to bear on Bida in anticipation of Jassim's arrival. He blasted many a building and caused the death of women and children, an event Jassim would never allow to be forgotten in the years following. Nevertheless, the fort came under heavy fire and its water supply was cut off. Mehmed had no choice but to appeal for a truce; he couldn't possibly report to Istanbul that his entire force had been wiped out. The Wali offered to release his hostages in return for the safe passage of his remaining cavalry and men out of Qatar and back to Hufuf. Mehmed, the very man who had presented the Sheikh of Qatar with the title of Kapucibasi four years earlier, had badly under-estimated Jassim's strength. The sheikh had not only repulsed an attack, but forced an Ottoman surrender. He had truly become a national hero, by far the most important political figure in the region. Qatar was no longer just a trail or grazing pasture for the tribes of eastern Arabia. On 26 March 1893 Qatar had been truly united. It was a country, and no mistake.

Jassim had always been a pragmatist; the victory was won but now he had to win the peace. Looking to restore the *status quo ante bellum*, he wrote to the Grand Vizier the very next day, laying out the injustices and misunderstandings which had led to the conflict. In part, Jassim hoped his explanations might temper the reports that, no doubt, Mehmed was firing off to the Porte from his base at Hasa.

> I sent Mehmed Hafiz Pasha my brother. But he sent him, along with other prominent members of this country, to jail. This attitude caused hatred among the people. I sent him word

to the effect that even a governor of the State could not act against the orders of the State. On the sixth day of the holy month of Ramadan, while we were in the desert, we were taken unawares. Certain tribes suffered losses, even women and children were not spared. In the face of all these events, the tribes had no other choice but to unite their forces to put up a defence. ... Under the circumstances, I humbly beg that an official be sent here to investigate the cruelties and oppression to which the people were subjected. It was Hafiz Pasha who compelled us to commit things we did not wish to happen and to retaliate.

Jassim's request for a fact-finding mission was initially accepted and the case was taken up by Said Effendi, a widely respected religious scholar based in Basra, who personally met Sultan Abd ul-Hamid II in April before travelling on to Qatar. He proposed reconciliation, but the Ministry for War in Istanbul felt that for all the benefits this might provide within the peninsula, it would give completely the wrong impression to tribes in the rest of eastern Arabia. Reconciliation would imply the Ottoman state was incapable of reprisal. It would imply weakness. And in the meantime, Hafiz's friends fought to have the investigation stopped before it started, afraid any incompetence revealed might end their career prospects. The Grand Vizier weighed in on the side of those working to prevent Said Effendi's mission, unreservedly recommending Mehmed Hafiz Pasha's account of the war to the Sultan and the necessity for ridding Qatar of Sheikh Jassim bin Muhammad bin Thani.

But despite all the pressure on the Sultan to use force, he instead demonstrated a genuine appreciation of the situation. Apportioning some blame to Jassim, Abd ul-Hamid II was clear on the point that the Qayamaqam should have presented himself at Bida when asked to do so by the Wali of Basra. The Sultan decreed, however,

Jassim had expressed his wish to be appointed Qayamaqam of
Qatar upon its capture in 1871 and has not since then shown
any mutinous behaviour. The British had claims of protectorate
over the Oman tribes in the environs of Qatar, the Muscat
Sultanate and the Bahrain Sheikhdom. Their intention to
extend the scope of these aspirations as far as Qatar should
not be a far-fetched conjecture. Under the circumstances, in
chastising the instigators of those incidents which took place
in Qatar, a more judicious and moderate action would have
been more pertinent. Consequently, instead of despatching
troops to punish them as the Governor of Basra seems to
suggest, it behoves us to clarify the matter in the first place
and unravel the motives for the dispute. Political and military
investigations must be conducted in the region, and according
to the result obtained they must be enlightened about the evil
consequences.

Jassim had got his investigation, to be managed by a committee
comprising Said Effendi, Colonel Rasim Bey and Mubarak Al
Sabah, the ambitious half-brother of the Qayamaqam of Kuwait.

In the meantime, London had got wind of the events at Wajba
and Bida and sensed opportunity. The torpedo cruiser HMS *Brisk*
arrived at Bida on 25 April, bearing a Colonel Adelbert Cecil
Talbot. Naturally, Talbot's mission was undertaken without any
reference to Ottoman officials, even though *Brisk* had anchored
right alongside the *Merrikh*, with Mehmed Pasha on board.
Mehmed was using the corvette as a base while he awaited the
Commission's questions with a due sense of dread. To end the
awkward stand-off, for neither recognised the right of the other
to involve themselves in Qatar's affairs, Talbot called on the Pasha.
He offered his own services in mediation between Jassim and
Mehmed. The Wali didn't hold back on the subject of Jassim,
and what he'd like to have happen to him, but the bottom line
remained: Qatari affairs were an internal Ottoman issue that did
not concern any British official.

Talbot hadn't expected any other response and sailed on to Wakra to meet up with Jassim, the main objective of his mission. Jassim was happy to accept the British invitation, and came aboard with his brother Sheikh Ahmad and Muhammad Abd ul-Wahhab. All were talkative and there was much to discuss. Describing in detail how the *Merrikh*'s shelling of Bida had killed scores of women and children in the town, Jassim stated that, at the age of 68, he wished for a peaceful life under British protection and intended to transfer his power to Ahmad, who would be based at Bida. The venerable sheikh continued that should he receive no justice after the investigative committee had concluded its work, he would personally lead an army to push the Ottomans out of Hasa and Qatif. The war had eaten into his funds and commerce had been badly affected. He was unable to pay the pearl divers their advance because the future was so uncertain. Sheikh Ahmad shared his brother's opinion, and suggested the 1868 agreement between Britain and Qatar have the dust blown off it.

In a telegram to Lord Curzon, the Viceroy of India, Talbot advised that Britain engineer a situation by which the Turks be invited to leave Qatar. 'Bida is at present deserted by Arabs, and will remain so unless their safety is assured ... I strongly recommend effort being made to procure their withdrawal and reinstatement independently of Qatar chiefs on footing of Trucial Chiefs.' Jassim, he added, was prepared to pay 9,000 *krans* annually to have the Ottomans stay out of the peninsula since their presence was ruining the country's prosperity.

Britain's foreign secretary, Lord Kimberley, was willing to enter into negotiations with Sultan Abd ul-Hamid II on the basis of the offer made by Sheikh Jassim and Sheikh Ahmad. But the suggestion was dismissed, and the Sultan expressed confidence that the commission he had established would resolve the dispute to everyone's satisfaction. The British interjection had the effect of spurring the Commission to greater haste. Mehmed Hafiz was dismissed, even before the Commission's findings had been published in June. The Ottoman relationship with Qatar, it proposed, should be re-established along the same lines as existed before the war. Jassim would pay his taxes, return the weapons he had captured and pass the Qayamaqamship to his brother Ahmad. In return, the Ottomans would facilitate the return of Bida's population and drop their plans for a customs house, among other administrative reforms. The Sultan accepted nearly all its recommendations, except for agreeing to Jassim's resignation, though he was happy for Ahmad to take over the day-to-day duties of the position. Jassim feigned a semi-retirement at Lusail for the first time, though it was a ruse which the British understood. A Major James Sadler, a temporary Resident in 1894, observed that Jassim 'probably finds it convenient for the present to interpose his brother as a buffer between himself and the Turks'. His perceptive observation did him credit. Jassim had won the peace.

Ottoman revenge at Zubara

Jassim had escaped the revenge of the Turkish bureaucracy in part by hinting at a British desire to make Qatar a protectorate, keenly aware that Ottoman policy was shaped by suspicion of foreign intrigue. London's hardening resistance to acknowledgement of Istanbul's sovereignty over the peninsula added body to the conviction, as did events on the ground. First, the Ottoman administrator in Bida and his wife were murdered by two Turkish soldiers a year after the peace. The perpetrators managed to escape only as far as Wakra before Jassim's men caught up with them. Secondly, and a year later, a huge migration from Bahrain saw Sultan bin Muhammad, a grandson of bin Turaif and the chief of the Al bin Ali tribe, settle in Qatar with over one and a half thousand followers. He had left Bahrain owing to a dispute with Sheikh Isa over a shooting. Sultan applied to Jassim for permission to settle in Zubara, which was given.

Sheikh Isa had never accepted the presence of any Bahraini

rebel in Zubara and appealed to the Political Resident to take up the issue. He insisted the Al bin Ali must return and impressed upon the political agent that the maritime peace was bound to break down if their settlement were allowed to prosper. The British agreed, and sent Colonel Frederick Wilson to Jassim that he might convey 'a strong and very distinct warning that such a settlement will not be permitted ... you must at once abandon any such project, which will not be tolerated. I confidently expect an early and satisfactory reply from you, as this matter will not admit to uncertainty or delay.' Britain had never accepted Ottoman authority, but now it was telling the Sheikh of Qatar what he could or could not do inside his own country, simply out of its concern that Bahraini shipping might be harassed.

Jassim was too experienced to respond directly to such attempts at duress, and wrote back merely that if Britain was no longer prepared to demonstrate 'friendship and good will', then their objections to Zubara's settlement should be taken up with the Sublime Porte. The reply had snookered Wilson, since Britain didn't recognise Ottoman authority in Qatar. The colonel decided therefore to browbeat Sultan bin Muhammad instead, assuring him that his men would be 'routed' if they didn't stop their constructions and return to Bahrain. Wilson also offered to mediate on the Al bin Ali's behalf to ensure they were not molested on their return. Sultan didn't have Jassim's political experience, and wrote back that he might consider leaving only after the end of the pearling season in early October 1895.

Wilson refused the delay, believing it was a ploy to buy time for the fort's repair. He had received intelligence that the new Mutasarrif at Hasa, Ibrahim Fawzi Pasha, had sent masons to Zubara, and even a detachment of soldiers. The British threatened to seize Sultan's pearling ships if he didn't acquiesce, but Jassim sought to reassure Sultan, helping him with the construction of houses and a mosque, and equipment for his fleet. A flagpole was erected specifically to raise the Ottoman standard, for this was exactly the kind of circumstance in which Jassim would welcome Turkish troops. Seeking to beef up their presence in Zubara, Jassim also called on his son-in-law, the Bahraini rebel par excellence Nasir bin Mubarak, and on the new Mutasarrif of Najd to march in support at once. Ibrahim Pasha did put in an appearance to review the situation personally, and promised on his return to Hasa to contact Basra on the need for soldiers and ships at Zubara.

HMS *Sphinx* cruised into Zubara in July. She was commanded by a Captain Pelly, who was under orders to seize all ships in the harbour should he fail to effect the town's abandonment. Pelly sent for Sultan bin Muhammad, who refused to come. A six-hour ultimatum was prepared and the captain ordered one of his men, John Gaskin – later to become the British political agent at Bahrain and a fluent Arabic speaker – to deliver it. As Gaskin was walking towards Sultan's house, two Ottoman soldiers blocked his path to ask by whose permission he entered the town. Gaskin replied that Britain didn't recognise Ottoman authority in Qatar and he would proceed within Zubara wherever he liked without reference to them or their superiors. A heated discussion followed and eventually the ultimatum was allowed to pass, but not the man carrying it. Gaskin returned to his ship while Sultan communicated to the *Sphinx* that he was no slave or subject to Sheikh Isa bin Ali, and though he could not contend against the power of the British government, 'no force or action on their part would compel him to return to Bahrain'. He added that both he and Sheikh Jassim bin Muhammad bin Thani had a few days previously written to Sheikh Isa bin Ali, and private negotiations were more likely to lead to their conciliation than threats from the British government, with which Sultan had nothing to do.

The ultimatum given, the twenty-gun sail and paddle steamer *Sphinx* swung into action, seizing eight Al bin Ali boats and conveying them to the Sheikh of Bahrain on 8 July. The Ottoman officer Arab Effendi protested to Pelly in writing, maintaining that Zubara was a part of Qatar and, therefore, the property of the

Ottoman state. The Al bin Ali, Effendi added, were the inhabitants of Qatar 'from ancient days, from grandfather to grandson. I do not understand your actions, this is contrary to all laws and usages; and if you have any reason for the same, negotiate with me and receive my reply and prevent your committing these injustices. If any of them [the ships] disappear and anything lost therefrom, you are answerable.' Meanwhile, Jassim had come in person to Zubara, and his presence gave the half-built town new hope. Sultan determined to continue in his resistance to such unjust demands and the Sheikh of Qatar offered genuine support. Advising the chief of the Al bin Ali to send his pearling ships round to Bida, on Qatar's eastern shores, Jassim also provided tents and camels to aid the tribesmen in their hour of need.

By mid-July, Pelly had returned from Bahrain and was on the hunt for more of Sultan's ships, chasing down nine more off the tip of the Qatari peninsula. Now Jassim attempted to reason with Wilson.

> I stood guarantee for them [the Al bin Ali] to Shaikh Isa that no mischief would arise from the side of Zubara or from its inhabitants, and they have committed no offence. They are poor who earn their livelihood; they are not slaves. Their original domicile was Qatar and they resided in Furaiha and Zubara, and then removed to Huwaila and Bida. They have not been ruled as slaves. This proceeding is contrary to your justice, and is a wrong unbecoming of you.

Pressed by Jassim, the Ottomans retaliated, responding to British hectoring by impounding nine Bahraini boats. Sheikh Isa had dispatched them to ferry those of the Al bin Ali who might wish to escape the tense situation and return 'home'. Pelly demanded to know by what authority the boats had been seized. Effendi replied with a didactic attempt at educating Pelly in the ancient history of the Al Khalifa and their migration to Zubara from Kuwait. Their conquest of Bahrain was made possible, he opined, by the contribution and sacrifices made by the major tribes of Qatar. Secondly, he pointed out, the Al Khalifa paid taxes and/or tributes to Qataris, particularly during the era of Rahma bin Jabir, and, therefore, Bahrain belonged to Qatar. Lastly, and by way of a side note, the Ottoman officer, who clearly had a flair for the historical but not for the political, asserted that both Qatar and Bahrain were parts of the Ottoman Empire. We'll never know whether Pelly made it to the end of Effendi's essay, but it hardly mattered, the situation had just escalated. The Ottoman navy had arrived.

There is much that has been written on the strength of the Royal Navy, and a veritable dearth of material on the Ottoman. This is a great injustice. While it is true that Admiral Ibrahim Pasha had lost the Battle of Navarino in 1827 during the Greek rebellion against Ottoman authority, it should be remembered that he had been fighting the combined fleets of the British, French and Russians, who had sent ten ships-of-the-line against his three. Two years later, Istanbul launched the biggest warship the world had ever seen – the *Mahmudiye*. Almost one hundred yards long, the *Mahmudiye* had 128 cannon mounted along three gun decks, manned by over 1,200 sailors. She was a true monster that belittled Britain's 74s. And even in the second half of the century, Istanbul was the first home for submarines that could fire torpedoes under water, in 1886. The truth is that the only thing the Ottoman navy lacked was a decent budget; their warships were the match of any in the world.

Once the Turkish gunboat *Zuhaf* had arrived, Pelly called for reinforcements. HMS *Pigeon* and the *Plassey* duly arrived. He had even requested a battalion of infantry from Bombay, but soon decided against landing troops. In the meantime, Jassim had called on Nasir bin Mubarak to bring his men and ships, and brought his own fleet to Zubara too. All the Qatari boats were flying Ottoman pennants and stationed themselves off the coast, from Ras Laffan to Fasht al-Dibal. Jassim was confident the British would not attack ships under the Sublime Porte's protection. Additionally, large numbers of tribal reserves, in the pay of the administration at Hasa, were also brought up to camp at Bir Jejim, in case any British marines attempted to land.

On 19 August, Ibrahim Fawzi Pasha issued an ultimatum giving Bahrain seventeen days to return the seventeen stolen boats, or else he would 'no longer restrain any Qatari tribe from attacking Bahrain'. This phrase has been dismissed as careless wording, but it is more likely that it was crafted deliberately. Arab Effendi had already told Pelly that Bahrain belonged to Qatar, something the Porte and Jassim had never claimed. But Ibrahim's ultimatum was interpreted as proof of Qatar's intention to invade, and the mischievous officer Effendi further sent a note to Pelly advising him to evacuate British citizens from Bahrain. Sheikh Isa needed little more convincing, certain that Jassim would move against Manama, Sultan and the Al bin Ali on Muharraq, Nasir and the Banu Hajir near Ras al-Barr and the Turkish military on Bahrain's west coast. This was manifest nonsense, albeit calculated nonsense. The government of India's resolve stiffened. Isa's predictions of imminent doom certainly had the intended effect in Bushire and London.

Under the command of Lieutenant Commander Cartwright, HMS *Pigeon* was sent to keep a strict watch on the movements of all the boats anchored off the eastern Qatari coast and report the slightest indication that tribesmen were boarding. The ship had inspected close to two hundred of Jassim's vessels, anchored off Ras Umm al-Hasa, when the Ottoman officer Arab Effendi stepped in to prevent the inspection, ordering the *Zuhaf* to facilitate *Pigeon*'s egression. Effendi's order indicated to Cartwright that something untoward was under way; an invasion force might well be preparing to board. Pelly sent Jassim a note, giving him one hour's warning of his intention to destroy the entire Qatari fleet.

At the same instant, the Ottoman gunboat *Zuhaf* left harbour. Arab Effendi took down the Ottoman flag and left for Hasa with his soldiers. Jassim was abandoned, left to watch as the harbour became a sea of fire. Forty-four of his boats were blown out of the water. Jassim applied for a truce to end the destruction, and asked that the owners of the surviving boats might be granted permission to take them back home to the ports on the west coast. Pelly replied he would consider ceasing hostilities if the Al bin Ali evacuated Zubara, the nine boats confiscated by the Ottoman Arab Effendi were returned and that the whole of Jassim's fleet be handed over as 'part security of any indemnity the Political Resident may levy upon you'.

By the end of September, Zubara was once again deserted. Sultan bin Muhammad couldn't face returning to Bahrain and thought to head for Basra. But there was no escaping Sheikh Isa. Sultan was shot by Majid bin Muhammad al-Dayaya, an Amamara sheikh, who boarded his ship at Ras Tanura in the night. Jassim attempted to appease the British, claiming he had assembled his fleet at the request of the Mutasarrif and had had no intention of invading Bahrain. Pelly wasn't convinced by the explanation, but observed: 'The Turks secretly desired that Jassim, whose effective subjection they have been unable to compass, and who inflicted a most disastrous reverse on their troops in 1893, should be crushed by being driven into a collision with British power.' The Ottomans had had their revenge. Jassim was without a fleet and without a means of generating revenue. His boats, over 140 of them, were taken to Bahrain. Pelly ordered they be returned only on payment of 50,000 rupees, which was later lowered by officials in Delhi to 30,000. Jassim didn't have such a sum of money and failed to meet the 17 February 1896 deadline stipulated. In any case, Jassim had never been the kind of man who responded to ultimatums. The boats were torched in Muharraq's harbour in May. It may well have been more merciful for the British to shoot the poor sailors whose livelihoods depended on the sea.

But the defeat held unexpected gains. The British government realised how close they had come to an armed conflict with the Ottomans, and wanted to make sure there would be no repetition of events. The Resident was consequently instructed to warn the ruler of Bahrain against interfering in the affairs of Qatar. This was, of course, an implicit recognition of the rights of the Al Thani in Zubara. At almost the same time, and with no more ships to lose, Jassim was determined to take control of Zubara and at least satisfy himself of the smallest of victories in what had proved a very bitter experience. The sheikh convinced those members of the Naim tribe who still lived near Zubara to move in and transfer their allegiance from the Al Khalifa to the Al Thani. This was no victory, but Jassim now controlled every town on the Qatari peninsula without exception.

A year after the incident, at the end of November 1896, the Ottoman embassy in London finally raised the issue of the destruction of Qatar's pearling and fishing fleet at Zubara. The insincere and half-hearted attempt at compensation was the final insult in the whole incident. The request received the briefest of responses from London: 'Her Majesty's Government consider that the measures in question were necessary for the defence of Bahrain which is under the protection of Great Britain.' Back in his youth, Jassim had expected that the Ottoman Empire, the Caliphate with over half a millennium of experience in protecting the Muslim world, would easily have offered the same kind of protection that Bahrain enjoyed under British treaty. He had been sorely disappointed and would never again accept their word as meaningful or honourable.

Ottoman incompetence was demonstrated again two years later, following a cattle raid by the new Kuwaiti sheikh Mubarak Al Sabah (who was about to sign a secret pact with the British). Mubarak had taken power in Kuwait after killing his half-brother, Muhammad, in cold blood in the early hours of 17 May 1896. After spending a lot of money on legitimising his usurpation, he looked to build up his wealth by any means whatsoever, including a raid on the Banu Hajir, who were under Jassim's protection. The

Ottomans at Hasa refused to intervene in the dispute between two Qayamaqams, though they had a clear duty to mediate. Jassim once again offered his resignation following an abortive attempt to retaliate. Istanbul refused it once more; Jassim quite simply ruled Qatar. To release him from his formal ties to the state would be to acknowledge his right to act as he pleased, and possibly deal with the British. But the decision not to accept the resignation was just as extraordinary, for Jassim encouraged the Banu Hajir to attack Ottoman troops in Bida in September 1899. A few people were shot on both sides. When HMS *Sphinx* anchored off Bida that winter, Sheikh Ahmad told her captain that Qatar desired to 'turn out the Turks and enter into agreement with the British government'. The Ottomans felt the growing pressure keenly, and sent an additional three battalions to Bida and kept the ship *Zuhaf* on coast patrols. But there was no coming back for the Ottomans as far as Jassim was concerned; their days were numbered. The question now was how to swap their 'protection' for a treaty with the British that recognised Qatari sovereignty.

10

SIBLING RIVALRY

THE POSTERS and advertisements of today date back only as far as 1870, the year printers finally perfected colour lithography and embraced what Sir Leo Chiozza Money would come to christen 'mass production'. Coincidentally, it was also the year Bovril was invented (which came within a whisker of being named 'Johnston's Fluid Beef'). Advertising would never be the same again. Graphic artists had the power to convince Joe Public they should buy Bovril for breakfast or get shot for Lord Kitchener. Oddly enough, however, it is not Alfred Leete's 'Your Country Needs You' and its multitude of spin-offs which can claim to be the world's most printed poster. The honour of designing an image instantly recognisable around the globe, and by far the most widely printed, goes to a rather studious Dutchman. Dr Herman Snellen was the professor of ophthalmology at Utrecht. His poster design is still the most sold in the USA today, 150 years after he drafted it with meticulous precision. It is displayed, along with its electronic descendants, in optometrists' offices, doctors' surgeries and various school sanatoria. It is, of course, the humble eye chart. Snellen's eponymous design became the global standard, providing a physical measure that could separate the normal from the myopic. The professor helped push back the frontiers of ignorance which surrounded poor vision and its treatment. Unfortunately, his work would not benefit a certain sheikh over three thousand miles away in eastern Arabia.

Jassim's eyesight was deteriorating quickly at the turn of the century. Age had been good to him on the whole, but all of his 75 years were beginning to take their toll. His friends blamed his myopia on his love of reading the Quran. As the condition worsened, he took to spending much more of his time with family and friends, in addition to keeping a beautiful farm at Lusail. He was relishing the far simpler existence after which he'd always yearned. At least, this was the image he projected to his occasional British visitors between 1898 and 1905, and there was much else to make his retreat into the country appear genuine. Though the Ottomans continued to refer to Jassim as the Qayamaqam, everyone knew their relationship was clearly at an end. The venerable sheikh must have sensed the impending doom of the Ottoman Empire and directed his attention instead to the future.

Thus it would be unwise to describe the first five years of the twentieth century as Jassim's retirement, or even semi-retirement. It was more a deliberate and disdainful divorce from all things Turkish. He viewed their presence as superfluous and enjoyed keeping Ottoman soldiers on their toes. The German adventurer Hermann Burchardt, who took the first-ever photographs of Qatar, observed in 1904 that local tribesmen levied taxes on Turkish officers for safe passage through Qatar's interior. At night, Turkish troops, he wrote, were living in a state of apprehension verging on terror. Sentries would man machine-gun posts rather than patrol the town they were supposed to be guarding. Even the Ottoman administrators seemed incapable of making the smallest decisions independently. When Burchardt asked for permission to use his camera around Bida, the *mudir* referred him to the Bin Thani.

Jassim could not run the day-to-day affairs of Qatar from

Lusail, however, and deputed the task to a brother who was 35 years his junior. Sheikh Ahmad bin Muhammad Bin Thani based himself in the capital, and worked hard to see Qatar become part of the Trucial system. In the absence of formal relations between London and Bida, this task was all the more difficult. It fell to Ahmad's political ingenuity to engineer an Ottoman exodus and enrol his country in the expanding British protectorate system sweeping up the coast of eastern Arabia. Both Jassim and he had flirted with the idea of pledging their allegiance to the British as early as 1895, so long as it was along the same lines as the allegiance of the other signatories – Abu Dhabi, Dubai, Ajman, Sharjah, Ras al-Khaima, Umm al-Qawain, Bahrain and soon Kuwait.

Ahmad was a great man in his own right, though he lived in his brother's shadow, providing immeasurable support to the Al Thani cause over seven years. His relationship with Jassim would come under strain a little in the last three years over policy and diplomacy, as we shall see. Sheikh Ahmad never resented keeping Turkish officials away from his brother's affairs, however, happy to act as a buffer between the two. The last British diplomat to see him alive described Ahmad as 'a somewhat extraordinary character and at the same time an extremely astute man ... who enjoyed much popularity and influence over his subjects'. He needed to be strong; the political situation that he inherited in 1898 verged on the untenable. He was 'in charge', but held no official position. He was neither the Sheikh of Qatar nor the Qayamaqam. The tribes looked to his brother; the Turks didn't trust any Al Thani and the British didn't want to change the status quo. In fact, the government of India was happy to see the Ottomans stay at Bida so long as they didn't try to do anything in any other part of the peninsula. It speaks volumes about Ahmad's personal abilities, therefore, that the Mutasarrif of Najd considered his authority 'sufficiently stable in nature' that he could be relied upon 'for controlling the Bedouins living in Qatar'.

Internal control was one thing, but external affairs were far more complicated. In the absence of a strong and authoritative Ottoman personality or naval presence, virtually all the maritime policing of Qatar's coast had come under de facto British control. For example, some of the Al bin Ali had moved back to Wakra and were pearl diving a few miles off the Qatari coast in June 1900 when five Amamara boats were suddenly blown into their midst by an adverse wind. Unable to believe their luck, the Al bin Ali gave the customary signal of battle by shooting at them. The Amamara boats replied with a fusillade of their own. Further action was prevented by the intervention of a nephew of Jassim. No one was hurt and the hapless intruders were allowed to leave without their weapons. Though Qatari justice had been served, the British political agent in Bahrain, John Gaskin, still saw fit to investigate the matter for himself, and ruled that the Al bin Ali must be fined 1,000 rupees, which was seized from their clansmen in Bahrain. The following year the Banu Hajir, headed by Salman bin Yetama, clashed with Abd ul-Hadi bin Mirait's ships off the shores at Dhakhira on Qatar's north-east coast. Again it was the British agent in Bahrain, John Gaskin, who resolved to deal with the case, and not the Mutasarrif of Najd. Gaskin would later refer the case to Sheikh Ahmad, which was convenient since Ahmad was keen to be communicated with.

Throughout 1902, Ahmad repeatedly pressed Gaskin to admit Qatar into the Trucial system. Unfortunately, his timing was most inopportune. For the previous eighteen months, Britain had pushed the Sublime Porte very hard over Kuwait, accepting Mubarak Al Sabah's desire for an alliance similar to the one sought by Qatar. In January 1899, Mubarak had secretly signed, pledging that Kuwait would never cede territory nor receive representatives of any foreign power without the British government's consent. In essence, London and Delhi now controlled Kuwait's foreign policy despite its status as an Ottoman territory under the control of the Wilayet of Basra. In total disregard of this fact, the treaty signed gave Britain responsibility for Kuwait's

national security in return for a mere 15,000 Indian rupees a year
– to be paid to the ruling family. That agreement led to what
has since been termed the First Kuwaiti Crisis, a heated political struggle between Istanbul and London, the Porte demanding
London stop interfering and London concerned it had weakened
the Ottoman Empire irrevocably in the face of greater colonial
competition from Germany.

Gaskin was loath to reply to Ahmad's request, though he and
his immediate superiors were both keen to accede to it. Despite
their best representations, London required that the status quo
around the Gulf be maintained for the time being. Ahmad mis-
interpreted the silence, however, and on 27 March proposed
that Qatar not only come under Trucial patronage but that men
and equipment be provided to ensure the swift removal of all
Ottoman forces from the old fort at Bida. It is a singularly incredible fact that not one Turkish officer or administrator had thought
to strengthen their position in the town. Ahmad revealed that
they had neither stockpiled supplies nor ensured their own independent control of drinking water. It hadn't occurred to a single
decision-maker, over the course of 30 years, that their base should
be redesigned, reconstructed or just moved so as to include a
well within its confines. The fort, as Jassim had proved ten years
earlier, was incapable of holding out for more than a couple of
days. It seems Turkish officers and their men banked solely on the
gunboat anchored at Bida harbour for their security. Despite their
weakness, it was only by June that Ahmad came to appreciate that
the British were not wary of the Ottoman garrison at Bida, they
were wary of the fallout from yet another Turkish defeat. Gaskin
dissuaded Ahmad from moving against the fort unless Britain
went to war formally with the empire. He also made it clear that
London would not extend its protection to Qatar, or even consider it, until after Jassim's death.

Following the loss of Kuwait, and nursing its wounded pride,
the Porte made one last desperate attempt at strengthening its

position throughout all of its territories in Arabia. In November 1902, the Mutasarrif was instructed once more to establish small administrative units at Zubara, Khor al-Udaid and Wakra. These repeated attempts to expand the area claimable as Ottoman, by appointing administrators to disputed settlements, were notable not only for their endurance but also for their total lack of effect. The state named *mudir*s to all three towns, intending or trying to install them for the next ten years. Since the British disputed Ottoman claims to sovereignty over the peninsula, they objected to the appointments, and no *mudir* remained at his post for long. Istanbul maintained its right of appointment, however, by continuing to name the officials (four to Zubara, six to Udaid and two to Wakra) even if they had to stay in Hufuf instead of at their posts. In at least one instance they tried to avoid British objection by assigning to Wakra a local notable, Jassim's son Abd ul-Rahman, first as *mudir*, then, when Britain objected, as a stipendiary of 'long standing'. But without Jassim's support, the plan was never likely to work.

Policy disputes

The term Wahhabi is used very freely these days and very often inappropriately. The Russian media, for example, use it as a term of abuse for Muslim activists in Central Asia and the Caucasus, as well as in Russia itself, rather than the vague and equally derogatory term 'Islamic fundamentalism' preferred in the Western media. In fact, the name is properly used to describe an Islamic revivalist movement which sprang up in the Arabian peninsula in the eighteenth century. They differed from their contemporary Wesleyans in Christendom in one major respect – Wahhabis had solid political backers and were not held back by the West's division between the secular and the spiritual. As is the case with so many revivalists in the course of history, Muhammad Abd ul-Wahhab, the founder of the movement, felt that the local practice of the religion had lost its original purity. The worship of graves and the veneration of saints were clearly prohibited yet had become common practice. The fledgling community of reformers found protection with the Al Saud clan, and the relationship endured. But never at any time did Abd ul-Wahhab's followers refer to themselves as Wahhabi. Even today, its adherents prefer the term Salafi, which links them to Islam's founding fathers, 'the pious predecessors'. But I have employed the word in the strict sense; Wahhabi here refers to the devout followers of the religious movement who attached themselves to the Saud family for support.

The Second Saudi State had come to an end after losing its struggle against the Al Rashid. The clan itself sought refuge in Kuwait. In a complete reversal of the 1991 Gulf War situation, it was Kuwait which helped the Al Saud revive their fortunes. Supplying weapons and men, a small band of steadfast warriors led by Abd ul-Aziz Ibn Saud made their way back towards Riyadh in 1902. Ibn Saud, the grandson of Faisal bin Turki, successfully assaulted the fort, killing the chief, Ibn Ajlan, as he was finishing the morning prayer. He then famously held Ibn Ajlan's head up over the battlements before tossing it to the people of city. The Al Saud were back, and many were pleased about it – most notably the 'retired' Sheikh Jassim.

Jassim immediately wrote to Ibn Saud to offer his congratulations to the grandson of an old friend and ally. The sheikh was already contemplating an anti-Ottoman alliance. As the years passed, Jassim had come ever closer to Wahhabi religious convictions and maintained contact with their protector, Ibn Saud, sending tribute, weapons and friendly assurances. He was fully aware of the effect his actions would have on the Ottomans, but did not concern himself with, or care to know, their view. He was more interested in gauging the impact this new alliance would have on his anti-Wahhabi nemesis, Sheikh Ziyad of Abu Dhabi. Jassim was excited at the prospect of change in 1902 and began to show all of his old vigour.

But Jassim's brother had no such ideological convictions, and began to chafe at an alliance being renewed without any reference to him – the man who had actually been trying to run Qatar over the last four years. You have to feel a little sympathy for Ahmad. He had always been seen in the subordinate position of deputy. Many an official would address letters to Sheikh Jassim for Ahmad to pass on, as if he were a messenger. The British wouldn't discuss a treaty until Ahmad inherited the sheikhdom. The Ottomans detested Jassim but still refused to bestow the title Qayamaqam upon Ahmad. Official visitors continued to pay their respects to Jassim instead of greeting him in the capital. This was the case in 1903, when Gaskin disembarked from HMS *Lawrence* on a mission to ascertain the mood in Qatar.

Gaskin met Jassim on 16 September at Lusail, where he and his immediate family had lived with two or three allied kinsmen and their families since the Battle of Wajba. The venerable sheikh maintained he had retired from government and transferred responsibility for its future welfare to his brother, informing the Ottomans that they should refer all matters to Ahmad before severing all connections. He now claimed to pay little attention to the actions of the Mutasarrif at Hasa. Gaskin's conversations with Jassim convinced him that the old fox was retired and disapproved of any Ottoman expansion inside Qatar, including his son's appointment as the *mudir* of Wakra. The truth, however, was that Jassim was not retired, and was in communication with the Al Saud and with Ottoman officials. He had pulled the wool over Gaskin's eyes with consummate skill for reasons that will become clear.

Gaskin's next stop was at Wakra to meet Sheikh Ahmad, who had confirmed the appointment of Jassim's son as *mudir* on a salary of six Ottoman lira per month, following the withdrawal of Yusuf Beg Effendi. (Jassim's son, Abd ul-Rahman, never took a single lira and refused to offer any guarantee of his future loyalty to the Porte despite Ottoman insistence.) This was the last occasion on which Ahmad would press to know whether Britain would offer its protection, and he warned that, if left to its own devices, the Ottoman Empire would absorb the whole peninsula and remove the Al Thani from power. Gaskin seemed to accept the argument, noting his prediction that the tribes of Qatar would soon disappear entirely because more of them had grown rich through pearl hunting, whereas they used to rely on the generosity of Jassim. The British official thus reported to his political agent that the Al Thani needed British support to enable them to maintain their hold over the tribes. Fortunately, his superior, Lieutenant Colonel Charles Kembell, was unimpressed. 'I am inclined to doubt if it is the case that the influence of the Al Thani family in Qatar is rapidly waning. It may, however, be less than it was ... What these people fear is the extension of Turkish rule over Qatar, as they know that they could not resist the Turks for long; and it is for this reason that the arrangement with His Majesty's Government is desired.'

Following the visit, Ahmad's patience with his brother was at an end. He didn't accept that an alliance with Ibn Saud was in the country's best interests, nor did he like Jassim's backing for an Ottoman expansion in various extremes of the peninsula. The appointment of the uncooperative, anti-Ottoman Abd ul-Rahman bin Jassim, against his better judgement, had weakened his standing with the Mutasarrif and now he was forced to devise a different strategy since the British, with whom Jassim no longer wished to align himself, were not prepared to offer their protection. This frustration would now turn into their first fraternal clash, which centred initially on the Turkish deployment of soldiers and administrators to Zubara, Udaid and Wakra.

Both men appreciated that the control of each settlement was at times a subject of dispute. Zubara was the focus of trouble with Bahrain, Udaid with Abu Dhabi, while the Al bu Aynain in Wakra were uneasy with the situation. But Jassim wanted, with or without their knowledge (he really didn't care), to use Istanbul's power to assert his position in the face of his British-backed rivals in Kuwait and Abu Dhabi. Ahmad didn't agree. He was set against any such Ottoman deployment. He believed it had been proposed in an attempt to increase control over entry points for smuggled guns and to stop use of these areas as bases for the Al Thani and their confederates. Ahmad's analysis was much closer to the mark. The year 1902 was, after all, a rare and prolonged period of attempting to establish the Ottoman flag around Qatar – the year of anti-British military reconsolidation elsewhere in Hasa, Yemen and Kuwait. The British were convinced it was Jassim who had asked the Porte to establish administrative units in those three places, had become suspicious of Ahmad by extension, and sent HMS *Sphinx* to try to prevent any Ottoman official from arriving at their new posts. Amid the confusion, it was easy for the situation to deteriorate and different tribes to back different policies.

Ahmad fared better in the low-intensity proxy war fought by his confederates, but Jassim would soon call upon his renewed friendship with the Al Saud to deal with his younger brother, who had never shared the same Wahhabi sympathies. In the summer of 1905, Ibn Saud was on his way to Qatar to resolve the differences between them and claimed he was acting under Ottoman authority. In reality he was coming to aid Jassim, whose supporters the Ajman had lost to his brother's backers, the Murra. But Ahmad couldn't afford for Ibn Saud to arrive, particularly as he knew Jassim had sent money and weapons to him for use against the ruler of Abu Dhabi, with whom both allies had quarrels of long standing. On the other hand, Ahmad couldn't be absolutely sure these weapons wouldn't be used against him either, and so decided to side with the Abu Dhabi sheikh and Ibn Rashid.

This change in alliance required Ahmad to hedge his bets, and so he decided to go on a charm offensive with the Ottomans, making some extraordinary proposals to the garrison commander at Bida. He attempted to repeat Jassim's success of 1871: gain Ottoman backing that could give decisive protection in a bid to become the internationally recognised Qayamaqam. Ahmad was now treating the Ottoman troops well and wanted to deepen the bonds between himself and the Sublime Porte. Detailing repeated British attempts to pry settlements away from Ottoman Qatar, he asked for the dispatch of fresh troops to block the schemes. Since he recognised that such a deployment might be difficult under present circumstances, Ahmad offered to pay for their transport or even supply enough money to support one or two battalions. In return he wanted public marks of Ottoman approval, including a rank and people to govern. In short, he wanted to become the Qayamaqam.

The commander was intrigued by the scheme. It could make control of Qatar immeasurably easier. With Ahmad's help the land could be run by about as many men as were now present in Doha; if the Saudi faction came to dominate in Najd and Qatar, no one could foresee the troubles that might ensue. He forwarded the request for troops and a ship to guard against the incursion of Ibn Saud. The question of the Qayamaqam title was more doubtful. While wishing to encourage Ahmad, the commander acknowledged that it would be impolitic to take the office from Jassim without a compelling reason. The best solution would be to give Ahmad a rank and make it clear to everyone that he would succeed his brother. The attempt at compromise gives a good indication of the Ottoman predicament in trying to maintain a legitimate claim of sovereignty over Qatar. It still depended on Jassim's goodwill, and there was little Ahmad could do about it.

But Ahmad was not ready to give up yet, and his support base was not insubstantial. In an apparent move to 'restore law and order' among the Bedouins on the south-western frontier of Qatar in April 1905, Ahmad led a raid with his Al Murra and Banu Hajir against Jassim's Ajman and Banu Khalid in Jafura, close to Hasa. Achieving no major success, the raiding party, which lost five men, returned to Qatar. Ahmad had come to the end of the line. He still managed to impose a semblance of order among the Bedouins on his south-west border, but his alliances were unravelling. Relations with the Ottomans were the first to fail when he unwittingly killed an Ottoman subject in September at Bida. On learning of his mistake, he expressed his regret to the Ottoman authorities and offered the usual blood money of 800 rupees, which was refused by the murdered man's relatives.

While Ahmad dealt with accusations of murder, the new political agent at Bahrain, Captain Francis Prideaux, had arrived in Qatar at the head of a delegation of interpreters, clerks, non-commissioned officers and an armed guard to collect information for the *Gazetteer of the Persian Gulf*, which was then under preparation. He was given money to purchase a Qatari horse to aid him in his travels, taking notes of anything that His Majesty's Government ought to know about Qatar. Once again, Prideaux didn't stop to talk to Ahmad but rather made straight for Lusail to meet the person who really mattered to them. Jassim received Prideaux well, and made him feel very welcome, answering his questions posed to provide copy for the *Gazetteer of the Persian Gulf*, to be written by John Lorimer, a British civil servant. But he made no effort to convince Prideaux that he desired an alliance of any kind. By the end of his stay at the farm, however, Prideaux was under no misapprehension, noting that nothing of any importance took place in Qatar without Jassim being consulted and giving his consent.

The Gazetteer of the Persian Gulf

Before describing Prideaux's meeting with Sheikh Ahmad, I simply have to tell you about Lorimer's 5,000-page monumental work, based on meetings such as those Prideaux conducted with Jassim. The *Gazetteer of the Persian Gulf* was designed as a practical reference book for British officials newly arrived in the Gulf. It told them why things were the way they were, and what was said about whom. It has some of the most fantastic gossip ever to have been written in an official government document. For instance, the Sheikh of Sharjah is described thus: 'In private life the Shaikh was weak, miserly and uxorious; in public business he was apathetic and seemed incapable of exertion. He alienated his subjects and former Bedouin adherents by indifference to their grievances and requests; and he forfeited the respect of the other Trucial Shaikhs by his general insignificance, both as a man and as a ruler.'

It gets even better, but before proceeding, it must be mentioned that the great weakness of its 'historical section' is that there is no attempt at viewing things other than through British official eyes. There is a bland assumption of the eternal wisdom and benevolence of imperial policy. And this was its great weakness. There is no suggestion that 'Hippopotamus' Murray, the British minister in Tehran, was an arrogant fool, even though the British foreign secretary himself, Lord Granville, observed that 'Murray's letters to the Shah are singularly offensive. His demands are quite absurd; yet orders are to be sent to occupy an island whose name I forget in the Persian Sea.' Instead, the *Gazetteer* presents the war as a just and necessary vindication of imperial prestige. This blatant jingoism allows Lorimer to write on 'the hostility of Sayyid Faisal towards British interests' as if this arose from some extraordinary vice in the ruler's character. There is no hint that he may have been goaded beyond his strength by the maladroit British agent, Major Fagan, whom Lord Curzon regarded as 'quite hopeless'.

A point essential to the understanding of the development of British policy in the Gulf in the early years of the century is totally omitted by Lorimer. There is no mention of the conflict between the expansionist urge of the government of India under Lord Curzon and the cautious line of the Foreign Office, unwilling to upset the status quo. For twenty years there was a divergence of views between successive viceroys and Whitehall ranging from the early days of the century over the proclamation of a formal protectorate over Qatar to the 1920s, when one side backed Ibn Saud and the other King Husain of the Hejaz in a civil war. Curiously enough these clashes of policy were regarded by French analysts, quite mistakenly, as yet one more ingenious triumph of the dreaded British Secret Service, which would always have 'its man in power whichever side won'.

The *Gazetteer* also omits matters of considerable importance. Lorimer does not say that the fat-headed action of Admiral Douglas in threatening to bombard Muscat in February 1899 (unless the Sultan publicly cancelled his cession of a coaling station to the French at Bundar Jissah) caused consternation in Whitehall. Again, there is no mention of the government of India's consideration of the use of force to prevent a Turkish occupation of the Kuwaiti-claimed island of Bubiyan in the spring of 1902.

But getting back to the gossip, the section dealing with Kuwait from 1902 to 1906 is hilarious; even the most apparently trivial matters find a place in it. The tome mentions, for example, the arrest of Sheikh Mubarak's representative at Basra on the charge of possessing an illegal newspaper and the pandemonium caused by Mubarak's unjustified claim to an unoccupied island. In the Bahrain section, some poor soul was sent to list all the chief features of the coast, then all the hills (four in number!), the villages (with numbers of huts), springs, tribal groups, boats (listed by ports), weights, measures and taxation. He tells us that there are 200 special white donkeys (the females are preferred as less noisy), 850 cattle (fed on dates, dried fish and old bones) and that imported goat meat costs 8 annas a pound. It is difficult to see what more information any man might hope for.

Sheikh Ahmad's demise

Following his meeting with Jassim, Prideaux sailed south down to Bida. He was keen to understand the sudden cooling in relations. Just a few years earlier, Ahmad had been anxious to bring Qatar under British protection. Ahmad gave a diplomatic response, claiming that although he still wanted such a treaty, he could do nothing to bring it about so long as the Ottoman forces remained in Bida fort. He asked, already knowing the answer, whether the British had any intention of evicting the Ottomans from Bida. Prideaux said it was impossible and may have felt he was the one blocking Qatar's inclusion into the Trucial system. In truth, however, it was Ahmad who had grown cold over the idea. The Trucial system in 1905 appeared to have broken down, or at least demonstrated that it was certainly not just an external protection agreement.

In the spring of that year, British troops had occupied Manama, the new administrative centre of Bahrain, using as a pretext the dispute which had arisen between a European citizen and a nephew of Sheikh Isa. London had taken over the administration of the island. The political agent had let the houses and property of the inhabitants they considered as offenders be looted in total disregard of Sheikh Isa; they seized the taxes which had been collected and the pearling revenue of the region. It was rumoured that Isa, who had until then claimed to be independent, had now started claiming to be a subject of the Ottoman government. Although this claim was insincere, the Sublime Porte decided to investigate the matter and act against Britain over the issue. This was enough to make any regional sheikh think twice about signing an agreement with Britain – it was a novel development that boded badly for non-interference on internal matters, but there was more. Mubarak al Sabah, the Sheikh of Kuwait, who saw danger in the face of a defection to Kuwait by certain traders in Bahrain, had attempted to close the British consulate in Kuwait. This move resulted in the British sending warships to Kuwait, threatening him with the loss of his position.

It seems that Ahmad would naturally have come to back Jassim's position with time, but unfortunately his time had just run out. In December 1905, Ahmad was murdered by one of his own men, a Banu Hajir tribesman who bore him a personal grudge. The speed with which Jassim now retook full control of Qatar clearly indicates his energy and confirmed Ottoman suspicions that he had never abandoned tribal politics in the seven-year 'semi-retirement'. It is ironic too that the British and Ottoman officials who had prepared various contingency plans in the event of Jassim's death had not stopped to consider he might outlive his younger brother. Jassim handled the emergency at Bida with his usual skill. Summoning the Banu Hajir to his camp, he made them promise that they would hunt down and execute the murderer. During the meeting one of the Banu Hajir notables was suddenly attacked and killed by a tribesman loyal to Ahmad. Jassim, up to the task, managed to calm the situation. Shortly afterwards Ahmad's murderer was caught and shot. The threat of a blood feud between the parties had passed. Jassim was back.

11

END OF AN ERA

D ISPLAYING ONE of the many mercury-induced eccentricities of his later years, Sir Isaac Newton once cut two holes into his front door. One was for the cat, he explained to incredulous guests, while the other was for her kittens. Such oddity tempers the exasperation he expressed in 1721, having just lost his fortune in the South Sea Bubble. Sir Isaac wrote: 'I can calculate the motions of heavenly bodies, but not the madness of people.' The aged bachelor had no money to pass on to his beloved niece, who had cared for him in his last years. Fate had spared Newton the difficulty of deciding who was worthiest to receive his legacy. Fate is rarely so kind.

The problem of bequeathing to a worthy descendant is a theme that dates back from well before the biblical parable of the talents. In more recent times, the eight paintings known as *A Rake's Progress* by William Hogarth explain – by use of the first storyboard known to history – the dangers of bequeathing to the unworthy. Published in print form in 1735, the eight pictures reveal the story of a Tom Rakewell, who inherits his father's fortune only to waste it and end his days in a prison and, eventually, a madhouse. Many cultures have recognised the inherent difficulties of bequeathing money or power. Some have sought to lessen the dangers by means of clever stratagems and systems. A couple of counties in eastern England practised ultimogeniture, whereby the youngest son would inherit all rather than the eldest. The Minangkabau indigenous to the highlands of West Sumatra only permit power, property and land to pass down from mother to daughter. And in pre-modern Kyushu and a few other areas of Japan, an estate might be apportioned among all sons, except that the youngest receives a double share as a reward for looking after his elderly parents.

Following the violent and unexpected death of his brother, the 80-year-old Jassim now had to consider who should take up his mantle. Throughout its history, Qatar had thankfully been spared much of the fratricide and civil war of the neighbouring sheikhdoms. Nevertheless, the process of passing on power in the peninsula's transforming society was fraught with difficulty. Traditionally, leadership in Qatar had been vested in a network of tribal chieftains, an elected leader in the sense of a *primus inter pares*. During Jassim's long life, a few eastern Arabian sheikhs had acquired additional power and prestige as a result of being recognised as Trucial sheikhs. Eventually, they adopted the title of hakim and finally, at independence, the title of emir, combining the attributes of ruler, commander and prince. This process, however, benefited only a few. The majority of tribal leaders under Jassim's rule had found their authority diminishing and, in many instances, disappearing entirely.

Jassim's choice of successor was made all the more difficult by another sea change which had also taken place during his own lifetime. The distinction between the nomadic, rural Bedouin and the settled, town-living *Hadar* had almost been lost. This was a major development, as Jassim was in many ways attached culturally to the former, much more so than his father, yet his rule had overseen the rise of towns. (And even when Jassim came to submit to the settled life in his twilight years, he still chose to do so away from the large population centres.) Throughout the

span of Middle Eastern history, the Bedouin and *Hadar* populations had maintained an unstable relationship characterised by
mutual need and mutual mistrust, each dependent on the other
while maintaining claims of superiority. The *Hadar* promoted
the civilised system by which a political succession was achieved
smoothly and peaceably and would allow access for discussion,
dispute and disagreement. From among these ideas was born the
majlis, a public session whereby the individual citizen was granted
personal access to the ruler and had an opportunity for immediate redress of his grievances. Another was the *shura*, the process
of consultation with community notables, an idea which would
eventually be incorporated into today's modern governments
through provisions for consultative or legislative assemblies. On
the other hand, the Bedouin had promoted a nomadic system by
which poor or bad leadership would be weeded out, and once
policy was agreed, all tribesmen were 100 per cent behind the
decision, with no regard for personal preference or opinion. It
was this factor which explains the tribe's great strength and its
great weakness. There was no permanent opposition that would
constantly argue with government. Decisions were made and
executed. It was not for tribesmen to question why, theirs just to
do and survive the best way that they could.

Jassim was thus to choose his successor at a time when the
establishment of coastal bases at Doha, Manama, Abu Dhabi,
Dubai and elsewhere represented a significant departure from
what he was used to as a youth or fully appreciated in his later
years. The act of selecting a permanent geographical centre had
resulted in an identification between the tribe and its settlement.
Furthermore, this shift from Bedouin to *Hadar* culture required
a concomitant increase in reliance on stronger political authority.
This was because the shift to permanent coastal settlement had
opened the way to greater contact with the outside world – pro-
moting an exchange of ideas and weakening the hold of traditional beliefs and customs regarding authority.

The concentration of political power in the hands of sheikhs owed a great deal to the activity of the British in the Gulf over the previous hundred years. Britain's supremacy over its southern shores was first manifested by the imposition of maritime restrictions on the Arab population, and assumed that each region must have one sheikh more powerful than others who exercised political authority over all residents of their settlements. In other words, their position was considered to be closer to that of hakim than the traditional conception of a tribal sheikh. But Jassim recognised that despite having achieved recognition of a sort by the British, the Trucial sheikhs received no benefit from this relationship as regards their internal position, nor would they until much later in the twentieth century. Thus it was that as Jassim came to consider the selection of a successor in 1906, he correctly perceived that any potential leader would still need to demonstrate some traditional qualities. He would need to depend on the vigour and speed he had displayed and the skill he could show in maintaining tribal support.

There were other factors that played significantly less on Jassim's mind as he came to consider the country's future. Although the foreign political relations of the peninsula were theoretically controlled by the Turkish military commander at Bida, the sheikh continued to act independently and with scant regard for such diplomatic sensibilities. For example, when Abd ul-Aziz bin Saud, son of the Wahhabi-aligned Emir, paid a visit to the districts bordering Qatar in 1905, Jassim sent a letter of welcome, with 8,000 German crowns in cash and a present of rifles and rice, and visited him personally at the wells of Uraiq. Jassim had long given up any pretence of benefiting from the 'protection' of the Ottoman Empire, but he was hopeful of establishing good relations with the Saudi state. The British had begun to take a much greater interest in the internal affairs of their Trucial allies, particularly in Bahrain and Kuwait. Retreating to his beloved farm in Lusail, Jassim was certain of only one thing. Bequeathing Qatar would be no simple task.

Choosing a successor

The venerable sheikh soon appointed his late brother's clerk, Ibrahim bin Salih bin Bakr, as Amir al-Suq for an interim period while he considered the succession issue. Despite the loss of Ali in Doha in 1888, Jassim still had eleven sons, only three of whom were experienced and old enough to be considered. But even these three worried him. He was concerned that the trio were too 'young and ignorant for the art of government'. Compounding the problem was that Khalifa, Abdullah and Abd ul-Rahman seemed loath to take up their father's responsibilities. Khalifa was content with his lot as Sheikh of Bida. Abd ul-Rahman was reluctant to accept his current position as the Sheikh of Wakra. The third, Abdullah, had become a wealthy pearl merchant in his own right and had no desire to deal with tribal disputes or Ottoman intrigues. Nevertheless, Jassim had narrowed his choice to one of these three, and wrote about the qualities he was looking for in at least one of them.

> The ruler of Doha should at once be both a soldier and
> a statesman, able to beat out the tribes and to march long
> distances whenever necessary, and while in Doha to keep
> order in the town, to remain conciliatory with the different
> tribes and to keep himself out of playing into the hands of the
> Turks. The Turks are powerless to do any harm when kept at a
> distance, but when close are difficult to manage.

The Ottoman garrison in Bida, headed by Major Nemit Effendi, appeared to recognise it had no formal voice, voting power or veto over Jassim's eventual choice. Nevertheless, it was concerned at the delay. After defeating Ibn Saud's forces in a pitched battle in June 1904, the Ottoman army in Hasa were suffering terribly from Ibn Saud's guerrilla reprisals. Major Nemit pleaded with Jassim to appoint a successor as quickly as possible, fearing tribal threats to his security and the possibility that even

Hasa province might fall, leaving his garrison isolated and unable to retreat except by sea to the nearest base in Basra. Major Nemit also urged Sheikh Jassim to accept the Qayamaqamship with a fixed salary, which the sheikh again refused to do. Nevertheless, as pressure mounted, Jassim intimated to the leading tribes of Qatar that they should help elect the next leader as soon as possible. The religiously inclined Sheikh Abdullah bin Jassim Al Thani emerged as the candidate of choice. Although he had initially declined the chieftaincy, owing to his stated interest in trade and commerce, various tribal missions eventually persuaded him to accept. By the end of the pearl season in 1906, Abdullah had became governor of Doha and Jassim's heir apparent. With encouragement from his father, Abdullah's first task was to launch a series of campaigns against unruly tribes as far as Salwa and Uqair. They met with success. Abdullah's diplomatic skills were tested too in November, when he restored harmonious relations between the people of Doha and the Ajman tribe.

Abdullah's first direct dealings with the British authorities in the Gulf were less auspicious, and soon became strained over the question of lawlessness on the Qatar coast. The Resident was certain that one Ahmad bin Salama had arrived at Doha in July 1906, after attacking a boat on the pearl bank. His presence at Doha had caused a good deal of anxiety among Bahrain's pearlers, even though it was highly unlikely he would commit any offence east of the peninsula. As usual, the British would not enter into communication with Ottoman officials in Bida as it would imply recognition of their authority. So the Political Resident, Sir Percy Cox, wrote to Jassim at Lusail directly, asking him to take action against Ahmad bin Salama and to instruct his dependants and Abdullah to have no dealings with him. Jassim and his son were treated to yet another display of Britain's self-appointed role as protector of peace on the Arabian Gulf.

> You are well-aware from of old time [sic] that the primary
> object of the British Government is to maintain absolute peace

and security on the sea, so that all the natives of the littoral may trade without fear. If persons in the position of yourself and your sons harbour and entertain the evil doers how can there be peace! Such conduct will bring trouble upon all.

The admonition had arrived while Jassim was visiting Ibn Saud in the Jafura desert, a few miles east of Salwa, much to the dissatisfaction of the Ottoman garrison. But Jassim had raced to Doha to protect his son's fledgling administration on learning that Cox had further chosen to deploy the six-gunned warship *Redbreast* off the Qatari coast on 10 September. Arriving at Doha, Jassim wrote in Abdullah's defence that Ahmad bin Salama had been given no welcome in Doha, and that his men had on the contrary attempted to apprehend the fugitive when he was spotted in the town at night. Jassim also insisted that the Turkish commander protest about the presence of the warship. It was enough for the present to ensure that HMS *Redbreast* withdrew, but clearly the venerable sheikh was concerned that, with no formal treaty between Qatar and Britain, such incidents were likely to be repeated. He was also worried that without any formal understanding between the Third Saudi State in Riyadh and London, Qatar might easily suffer in any confrontation between the two.

Fortunately for Jassim, his meeting in the Jafura desert had borne fruit. Ibn Saud wished him to broker a political understanding between London and the Third Saudi State. If he were capable of establishing Anglo-Saudi relations on a solid foundation, it would leave Qatar indirectly protected by the British – since all other parties in the southern Gulf would be under an obligation not to invade their neighbours. Jassim secretly sent an urgent letter to the British agent in Bahrain, Francis Prideaux, through Sultan bin Nasir al-Suwaidi, head of the Sudan tribe of Bida, expressing his earnest desire to meet him at Lusail 'just for a quarter of an hour', without disclosing the agenda of the proposed meeting. Jassim himself had written and signed the letter. But Prideaux was wary of attending, and sent his interpreter to the meeting on 23 October. Although there is no record of the words spoken at the meeting, it became clear that Jassim had been asked to speak on behalf of Ibn Saud regarding British protection. This was an account of the message delivered by the interpreter back at Manama.

> The resources of Najd are stated to have been strained to the utmost by the recent internecine wars, and Ibn Saud considers that the oases of Hasa and Qatif were always the most profitable possessions of his Wahhabi ancestors. He is anxious therefore to recover the two districts and he proposes that a secret understanding should be arranged between the British Government and himself under which he should be granted British protection from Turkish assaults at sea, in the event of his ever succeeding in driving the Turks, unaided, out of his ancestral dominions. In return for this protection the Amir is willing to bind himself to certain agreements (probably similar to those of the Trucial Chiefs) and to accept a Political Officer to reside at his Court. The details of his secret treaty he wishes to be settled or discussed at an interview which he is ready to give Prideaux either in person, or with his brother representing him, at some convenient rendezvous in the desert.

Jassim wanted the reply to be given to him 'only by word of mouth'; he would arrange to forward it to Ibn Saud by 'trusted messenger'. Prideaux, however, was against such a secret agreement with Ibn Saud in view of Britain's troubled relationship with the Ottoman government. The authorities in the Gulf therefore sent no immediate reply to this representation. More than eight months later, however, Prideaux was instructed to tell Jassim that the British government was unable to entertain his proposal for Ibn Saud's protection as British interests were 'strictly confined to the Coasts of the Gulf'.

In the meantime, Qatar was experiencing a severe economic depression owing to the lack of rainfall. For want of winter grazing and the unseasonably hot weather in 1907, most of the nomadic tribes of Qatar were obliged to send their sheep, camels and horses to Hasa. Economic conditions in Qatar deteriorated further as the demand for the country's only export – pearls – evaporated too. No one was set to lose more than Jassim himself; he had invested well over a million Indian rupees. He sent Abdullah to Bombay on 13 April to investigate the collapse personally. Abdullah stayed more than three months, but managed to sell none of his own or his father's stock, even after lowering the price considerably.

The depreciation of pearls hit the Al Thani income hard, Jassim had to establish a customs house in Doha under the administration of one of his servants, although everyone was opposed to the move. The sheikh was no less loath to establish the tax – after all, opposition to such a tax had been one of the prime motives in his decision to fight the Turks – but the state had lost 50 per cent of its revenue in one year. But the customs house failed to boost finances and the pearl market remained depressed for two years. The elite of Qatar were all on the verge of bankruptcy, though this did not affect them as severely as it would those in other parts of the world. Most had experienced an extreme poverty that would make Oliver Twist's early life appear exuberant by comparison. In any case, Qatar's creditors among the general population had no effective means of redress. In such circumstances, it is easy to appreciate that the new tax on shipping was not well received, and Jassim's son at Wakra, Abd ul-Rahman, began to feel the wrath of the Al bu Aynain. By September 1908, many were refusing to pay the annual tax levied on their pearling boats. Abd ul-Rahman responded by imposing a fine of 10,000 rupees on the tribe and, when they refused to pay, expelled six of their notables from Wakra.

It is astonishing how seemingly minor issues are welcomed by empires as an opportunity to conduct their pre-planned business. Robert Jenkins was as amazed as fellow contemporaries that his pickled ear, seven years after it was cut off, provided the pretext for a nine-year war with Spain. No one could have imagined the assassination of Archduke Franz Ferdinand would lead to the death of well over ten million people. More recently, it seems that an unproven claim regarding the possession of weapons of mass destruction was a good enough reason to invade Iraq, with its many unforeseen consequences still unfolding. So it was that Qatar's regional dispute over tax was soon debated in imperial parliaments, attracting their unwanted interest, even after the minor event at Wakra had been resolved amicably. It seemed that both the Ottoman and British empires were determined to escalate a series of high-profile confrontations. By December 1908, three members of the Al bu Aynain tribe of Wakra had paid a visit to Mahir Pasha, Mutasarrif of Hasa, and informed the Pasha that the tribe had settled their difference with Jassim and abandoned their calls for the establishment of an Ottoman military post.

Nevertheless, owing to the tribe's connections with Bahrain, Prideaux took the opportunity to visit Jassim at Lusail, to discuss the 'problem': the Al bu Aynain tribesmen had appealed to the Ottoman Wali of Basra for protection, sending one of their kinsmen, Ahmad bin Khatan, as an envoy to request that an Ottoman military garrison be established in Wakra. The Wali, Muhurrem Pasha, had written to Jassim asking him to settle the dispute peacefully, but also told the Al bu Aynain that they too should apply to the Mutasarrif of Hasa for assistance against the Al Thani. In the meanwhile, the British consul at Basra learned of the Wali's interview with the Al bu Aynain's envoy and warned Muharrem that 'His Majesty's Government does not recognise Turkish sovereignty on the Qatari peninsula' and no Ottoman interference would be allowed in Wakra. The consul, Francis Crow, reminded the Wali that his intervention in the affairs of Wakra was contrary to the Porte's previous instructions to abolish the mudirate of Wakra and not to interfere there.

Crow's note, however, created uproar in Istanbul. On 25

July 1908, the Ottoman Ministry of Foreign Affairs rejected the British assertion.

Ottoman sovereignty over the Qatar peninsula definitely exists. Jassim bin Thani, a Qatari citizen, in his official capacity as Qayamaqam appointed by the Sublime Porte, is in charge of the administration of tribes and of ensuring safety and order in the place. He, together, with the *naib*, his deputy, along with the administrators at Zubara and Udaid and other districts, are on the payroll of the Ottoman State. Jassim affixes his signature on official papers in this official capacity of Qayamaqam of Qatar. A flawless civil administration and the presence of a military power consisting of a battalion and two artillery units in Qatar are sound evidence of Ottoman sovereignty. Abd ul-Rahman Effendi, son of Jassim, appointed administrator to the district of Wakra by decision of the administrative council, is now discharging his duty.

The British response came quickly. Bahrain was warned that Ahmad bin Khatan and his fellow tribesmen should be censured; their mission to Basra to solicit Ottoman troops for Wakra was highly inappropriate. Henceforth, no Bahraini subject should be permitted an opportunity to 'carry the grievances of their kinsmen or encourag[e] the latter to represent them to the Turkish authorities or other foreign Governments'. And even though the Wakra 'crisis' had been solved thanks to Jassim's personal intervention, Prideaux wanted to make sure no Ottoman official ever had a pretext to deploy in Wakra again. He anticipated that the tribe might still leave Wakra to avoid tax and further direct confrontation with Abd ul-Rahman. If this happened, the Ottomans, merely by threatening to intervene, would 'bring the Al Thani to the point of conciliation where the tribesmen would meet them', thus making good use of the opportunity to increase their authority in the Qatar peninsula. To avert such a possibility, Prideaux had already written to Sheikh Jassim on 30 January 1909, expressing his desire to meet him at Lusail, Abu Dhaluf or Fuwairit.

Conspicuously absent from the three suggested venues was Doha or Wakra, for fear of attracting Ottoman attention. Agreeing to meet in a month's time at Lusail, Prideaux was once again informed that the Al bu Aynain problem at Wakra had been solved. He attempted, however, to draw Jassim's attention to an alleged Turkish plan to assume the administration of the Doha customs. This was unlikely, and the adroit Jassim replied that, even if this were true, the revenue from this source was very meagre, amounting to only 400 rupees a month. Such a revenue was insufficient even to defray the cost of the officials needed to run it. No sooner had Prideaux failed in encouraging Jassim to raise tension on the back of Wakra than the Ottomans attempted to do the very same thing in Wakra itself. With Mahir Pasha's backing, a thousand members of the Al bu Aynain, headed by Abdullah bin Ali, were encouraged on 5 October 1909 to leave Wakra for Qasr al-Subaih, a town on the mainland about thirty miles north of Qatif which was under Kuwaiti control. Initially Sheikh Mubarak extended all kinds of assistance, including supplying food, but soon came to realise that they were now agents of the Wali of Basra and the Mutasarrif of Hasa, and would remain so until Ibn Saud forced the Ottomans out of eastern Arabia.

Zakhnuniya

Despite the mass emigration from Wakra, neither the British nor the Turks were able to find the spark that would ignite a full-scale diplomatic confrontation, though it was as if both sought it. This would change soon. In March 1909, while British attention was focused on the increased trade in arms, Istanbul encouraged the *mudir* of Uqair to occupy a tiny desert island, which had no permanent population but a broken-down fort, 10 miles to the south of his town. It was called Zakhnuniya. The new spurt of energy was due to the change of government in Istanbul, following the overthrow of Sultan Abd ul-Hamid II by a combination of army officers and young bureaucrats. The revolution was part of what came to be known as the Young Turk movement, the main aim of which was nothing less than the salvation of the Ottoman Empire through restoration of the constitution of 1876, curtailing the power of the Sultan. The revolutionary regime brought a new dynamism to the politics of Arabia and posed, for the last time, as a genuine power with which to be reckoned. The British ambassador in Istanbul, Sir Gerald Lowther, was convinced that more Ottoman naval units would soon be cruising the Gulf as the fleet had been augmented by German-built ships. As the presence of more Ottoman ships in the Gulf would increase Ottoman influence, Lowther advocated sorting out unfinished business in Qatar, the only littoral country which remained outside the British Trucial system of administration, so as to prevent any possible Turkish toehold in the Gulf.

The island was frequented only by the migratory Dawasir tribe during the winter fishing season. The Bahraini-built fort, where the *mudir* hoisted the Ottoman flag, was almost in ruins. It had been abandoned for almost forty years. Nevertheless, the *mudir* claimed the island in the name of the Sultan Mehmed V, a mere puppet of Talaat Pasha – whose distressing policy towards Armenian citizens is still capable of provoking debates in the US and French senates 100 years later. The four soldiers who helped conquer Zakhnuniya told the few Dawasir to be found that they should recognise themselves as Ottoman subjects. The Dawasir men may only have been humble fishermen, but they were no fools and declined to accept the gracious offer of citizenship, arguing that they would most likely lose their possessions in Bahrain if they obliged. Despite this slight shower on his parade, the *mudir* nonetheless could return home proud to have done his duty. He would have been in no doubt that Britain could not let the 'invasion' of Zakhnuniya pass unanswered.

Sure enough, Britain interpreted events in the most dramatic way possible. Zakhnuniya was claimed by Bahrain, and its occupation each Friday by some day-tripping Turkish patrol raised the question not only of British protection over Bahrain but of the limits of Ottoman jurisdiction on the Qatar coast. It constituted, therefore, no less than a clear breach of the status quo that Britain was determined to maintain. Prideaux proceeded to the island on 18 March, which was a Thursday, to take stock of the situation. But he had arrived a whole day ahead of the weekly invasion force, and so found only one fishing boat on the beach on the west side of the island. He had noticed, however, a flag of suspiciously Ottoman appearance carefully rolled up and fastened tight to a flagpole. From Zakhnuniya, Prideaux proceeded to Hawar island, about one mile off the west coast of Qatar, which had been a dependency of Qatar from time immemorial. Here he found two winter villages consisting of 40 large huts belonging to the Dawasir and under the authority of one Isa bin Ahmad Dawasary – who considered himself independent of both Bahrain and Qatar.

Keen to prevent any Ottoman attempt at claiming a single Hawar island, Prideaux now urged Bahrain to make a claim just to avoid a Turkish takeover. 'I strongly deprecate letting the Turks keep Zukhnuniya, as they will then naturally be encouraged to go on to Hawar, but if Shaikh Isa doesn't want or dare to assert his sovereignty over Hawar we shall be in rather a quandary.' But Sheikh Isa of Bahrain was not interested and made no such claim, satisfying himself by stating on 30 March 1909 that Zakhnuniya belonged to him as his father had built the fort there 50 years ago and his subjects periodically resided there in order to fish. Delighting in Britain's irritation, the Mutasarrif of Hasa now sent 60 soldiers and four field guns to Khor al-Udaid, which Britain claimed belonged to Abu Dhabi. Jassim had no intention of intervening, content to sit back and allow the Ottomans to extend Qatar's borders. At one point, Britain considered landing Indian troops. But events elsewhere in the Gulf would once again change the situation. Before long, the Ottomans backed down, withdrew their *mudir* from Udaid and agreed to abandoning Zakhnuniya. Istanbul had a lot more to gain from a new power entering the Gulf for the first time. German power had arrived.

Qatar achieves autonomy

While Nostradamus enthusiasts will no doubt find that the French apothecary had in fact written a quatrain predicting Germany would actually help bring about the last stage of Qatar's journey to independence, Jassim and his fellow countrymen were blissfully unaware of the Anatolian Railway Company and its grand designs. Established in 1888 by two German financiers, Herr Kaula of the Wurtembergische Bank and Dr George Siemens, the director of the Deutsche Bank, the Anatolian Railway Company planned to construct a route from Istanbul to Ankara. Their experience in the United States, where they had personally witnessed the opening of the Northern Pacific network by the former president Ulysses Grant in 1883, had inspired them. Within in a decade they had the capital and the political clout that would allow Baron von Marschall von Bieberstien, the German ambassador to the Sublime Porte and staunch nationalist, to persuade the Turks to extend the line all the way to Baghdad.

The scheme's main objective was to exploit the Ottoman markets as an outlet for its own rapidly growing industry. The Ottomans were equally keen as it would enable them to supply their eastern colonies with far greater ease and speed. But Britain was very concerned. It was Von Marschall who had declared in the Reichstag that the maintenance of the independence of the Boer republics in South Africa was a German interest. He was also an advocate of a strong naval policy for Germany and exponent of Berlin's resolute opposition to any practical discussion of the question of restriction of armaments. He was exactly the kind of man who would recognise the value of extending the railway to Kadhamah in Kuwait, the best harbour in the entire Gulf and the most suitable place for a military base. The British were in a difficult position; London still had not made public its secret Trucial agreement with Kuwait signed almost a decade earlier.

London came up with two policy directives to thwart German expansion. First, it started buying up huge tracts of land along the Kuwait coast, and secondly, it prepared to come clean about its secret deal with Kuwait and so clear up who governed what in the Gulf. On 29 July 1911, the British Foreign Office informed Haqqi Pasha, the ambassador in London, that Kuwait was in fact under British protection and proposed that ownership of the railway should be split into 20 per cent shares for the Turks, Britain, France, Germany and Russia. The letter also urged Istanbul to recognise Britain's absolute right to police the Gulf, and thus the Porte should renounce its claims to Qatar. Negotiations began, but stopped over the Agadir crisis, or Panthersprung, off the coast of Morocco. This was the first time Germany would challenge British naval superiority, in July 1911. Two months later and the Ottomans suffered the outbreak of the Tripolitan war, when their troops would be the first in history to experience bombs dropped from enemy aircraft and dirigibles. When negotiations restarted, Qatar was the one sticking point, and the Porte suggested joint jurisdiction. But London would not accept. Sir Arthur McMahon, the Foreign Secretary to the government of India, wrote most passionately on the subject. 'Turkish ownership in Qatar will give them for the first time in history a foothold in the Arabian Gulf with many potential possibilities of development, not only in the interior of Arabia but in regard to the Gulf itself, which will in time enable her to claim the right of intervention in Gulf matters of which we desire to retain a monopoly.'

After much horse-trading that lasted until 7 April 1913, the Ottomans agreed to withdraw their troops from Qatar entirely, on condition that the peninsula remained autonomous. The government of India also cleared the way for Qatari autonomy, stating that the Turkish proposal was acceptable on condition that the autonomy should mean 'complete renunciation of all claims to suzerainty on the part of Turkey' and Britain should have the right to conclude necessary agreements with Qatar to 'secure maritime peace or suppression of illicit arms traffic'. Britain also agreed, once more, to stop Bahrain attempting to annex any part of the peninsula. The agreement held even after Ibn Saud conquered Hasa province in May 1913, though it meant that London and Istanbul had come to an arrangement without any regard to Riyadh, which was now in the forefront of Gulf politics. (The Turkish garrison at Bida found itself in a sea of hostility, and would end its days in ignominy. Most soldiers would desert, escaping to the Persian coast. The last few officers and men left when HMS *Pyramus* arrived on 20 August 1915 during the First World War.)

It fell to British political agent Sir Percy Cox to inform Jassim on the particulars of the Anglo-Ottoman Convention in June 1913. Cox had planned to ask the Sheikh of Qatar permission for a British agent – who would be Muslim if he preferred – to be allowed to settle at Bida, along with a new Banyan community. Some of Cox's requests were more demanding, such as a promise from Qatar to permit only British or Turkish officials to correspond with him, in a bid to keep Ibn Saud and possibly even the Kaiser at arm's length. But it is fair to guess Jassim would have welcomed the agreement as a realisation of his life's work – Qatar's independence.

But the 88-year-old Jassim passed away peacefully in his sleep on 17 July 1913. Prideaux had once described him as the 'patriarch of ancient times', but in reality he was the father of a new nation-state. The towns of his birth, which had almost been seasonal, were firmly established. The tribal and sedentary communities were fused irrevocably. The first purpose-built roads and schools had been established. The Ottomans had been defeated and pushed out. The peninsula's borders were recognised by the greatest powers of the day. Qatar was a nation–state and the authority of its next ruler was established and accepted.

Qatar's total independence would last three years. In 1916, Jassim's son would embrace the protection afforded under the Trucial system. Abdullah did not share his father's relationship with Ibn Saud, who was looking ever more closely at Qatar. Britain had played on his anxieties, with the Resident exclaiming: 'I have not a doubt that Ibn Saud could eat up Qatar in a week and I am rather afraid that he may do so.' Nevertheless, when Jassim was buried at Lusail, it was Qatari sand which was poured into his grave. He was buried then as the father of a nation, and is honoured as such today, and will be for ever.

CONCLUSION

QATAR LOST a great leader and a great man on 17 July 1913. In his lifetime, Jassim had such an invigorating effect on his own society that it was easy to forget what daunting historic tasks he had set himself. He sought and succeeded in forging an independent nation where none had ever existed. He did this in the face of an ever expanding imperial world, while freeing his own people from disunity and insecurity. When asked sarcastically by a petty British official whether any other Bedouin expended so much energy in opposition to the British, Jassim replied that no two Bedouins' combined efforts could equal his own.

His was a cause hard to accomplish and heavy with risk. Yet it was pursued with selflessness, and an almost naive openness and simplicity. On 3 May 1881, Jassim wrote to Britain's Political Resident in the Gulf, stating: 'Qatar is not the property of anyone, except of him who inhabits its land and guarantees its peace ... we and the people of Qatar have more right to it [than you].' He was also capable of the most personal sacrifices, even divorcing his wife, Jafla – the mother of his son Abd ul-Rahman – in a successful bid to settle a blood feud between the Al bu Kuwara and Amamara tribes. (Jafla was of the Al bu Kuwara.)

In the terrible weeks following the murder of his son by tribesmen from Abu Dhabi, it was no accident that both Abd ul-Rahman bin Faisal and Ibn Sabhan of the Rashid chose to join him from hundreds of miles away in his search for retribution. He was well liked; even his enemies held a grudging respect. Whether for his obvious affection for his grandchildren and his farm, the annual family retreats into the desert or, as copies of his will demonstrate, support of charities and education around the Arabian peninsula, there was a genuine and popular affection too. The crowds that gathered in Bida to welcome Jassim home following his year in a Bahraini prison were unprecedented. As he unveiled the Qatar-red flag for the first time, Jassim's ride out of Bida with a cavalry unit to face one of the most feared warriors in eastern Arabia is the stuff of Hollywood film. Even Jassim's enemies recognised his strength and willingness to raise himself above tribal disputes. Thus it was that the Naim came to him for help when their leader had been imprisoned by the Al Khalifa in Wakra.

It is hard to deny that Jassim's life was providential, when we look at what he achieved in his 35 years in power. Qatar cannot be said to have had a national economy, but the standard of living in 1910 was a major improvement on that of the 1870s. Although it would be left to Jassim's son for Qatar to see its first paved roads and telegraph wires, tribesmen and trader alike accepted that they belonged to something bigger than the tribes and towns of their forefathers.

While Jassim respected his father greatly, he did not blindly follow his policy and was bold enough to take steps no other leader in the Gulf would consider. Expelling every single Banyan from Bida, for example, was something no other leader would dare contemplate, let alone emulate. His refusal to submit to British coercion, as illustrated by the burning of the nation's pearling fleet in the 1890s, showed that he was prepared to sacrifice everything rather than submit to foreign authority. His defeat of the Ottoman army at Wajba, in the same decade, clearly demonstrated that there were basic principles of freedom over which he would never compromise.

This independence of spirit manifested itself early on in his life. He always chose to wear a different style of dress to that of his father from a young age, adopting the Bedouin clothes of the Najd. His father had attempted to have Qatar become part of the Trucial coast under British protection. But Jassim had the vision to convince his kinsmen and confederates that it was better to benefit from Ottoman protection, even as the Sublime Porte was falling into terminal decline. Others saw only limits to his policy; but Jassim ultimately founded the only independent emirate in the Gulf.

Perhaps what is most clear is that Jassim knew his own mind. He had firm principles, expounded them clearly and acted upon them decisively. Some historians have called this stubbornness, but I think anyone who has achieved anything worthwhile has to be stubborn. Despite his admiration for the Wahhabi ideals expounded in the various Saudi states, Jassim was knowledgeable on Hanbali jurisprudence and gave the *khutba*, the Friday sermon, at the main mosque in Bida. His generosity was even recorded by his many British visitors. When empires threw problems at him, he was not baffled, or disoriented, or overwhelmed. He knew almost instinctively what to do simply because he had a wealth of experience. He had not become the Sheikh of Qatar until the age of 53.

In the three years following his death, Abdullah bin Jassim (ruled 1913–49) took up his father's mantle. He had been reluctant to accept the position, perhaps even a little intimidated, and was more inclined to remain a successful pearl merchant. But Jassim chose him from his twelve sons, all of whom deferred to their father's wishes. Amazingly, Jassim had one trick left to play. Four days after his demise, the ruler of Bahrain, Isa bin Ali Al Khalifa (ruled 1869–1932), tried to revive his claim to levy taxes on Qatar according to the treaty of 1868. Isa was shocked to find that Jassim had prepared for such a contingency, and the British informed Isa that, according to a treaty agreed between Jassim, the Sublime Porte and Britain: '*Le Gouvernement de sa Majesté Britannique declare qu'il ne permettra pas au cheikh de Bahreine de s'immiser dans les affaires intérieures d'El Katr.*'

The story of Qatar has continued in dramatic fashion. Following the crash of the pearl market, the Great Depression and the discovery of the second-largest natural gas reserves in the world, the nation is no longer unknown or obscure. It owes its foundation to Jassim, who was as good as his word.

> I lifted injustice for no personal gain
> but to see the weaker freed again.

LINE OF DESCENT OF
RULERS OF QATAR

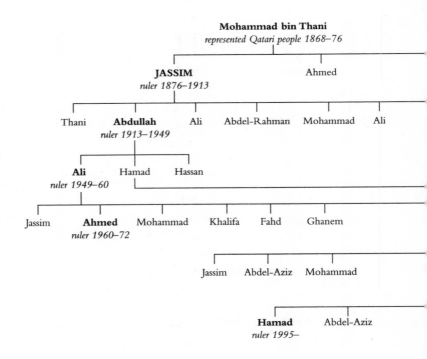

Mohammad bin Thani
represented Qatari people 1868–76

Ahmed

JASSIM
ruler 1876–1913

Thani   **Abdullah**   Ali   Abdel-Rahman   Mohammad   Ali
ruler 1913–1949

Ali   Hamad   Hassan
ruler 1949–60

Jassim   **Ahmed**   Mohammad   Khalifa   Fahd   Ghanem
ruler 1960–72

Jassim   Abdel-Aziz   Mohammad

Hamad   Abdel-Aziz
ruler 1995–

Line of descent of rulers of Qatar

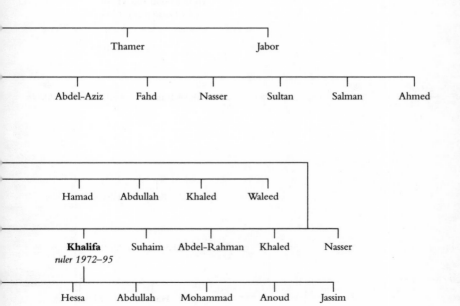

GLOSSARY

'aqal – the band that keeps the headdress, or *gutra*, on
archa – a dance performed by men, originally a war dance
baghla – a Gulf-built transport ship
barkhan – full-size, crescent-shaped dune
barr – stony desert
bateel – a medium-sized Gulf-built vessel, sometimes used
  for military purposes
birag – hills forming a scarp, capped with limestone
boom – the largest of the Gulf-built seagoing vessels
buhur – literally meaning seas, it is also used to describe
  poetic metres
dahl – a subterranean cavern containing water
dhahr al-khait – the windward side of a dune
dira – all the land that comes under the authority of a
  particular tribe
diwan – a book containing a poet's collected works
doha – a bay
fijeeri – songs, or shanties, sung by pearlers
gehaab – wind-eroded hills in the east
ghaws al-barid – the first part of the pearling season
ghaws al-kabir – the main part of the pearling season from
  May to September

ghuri – a fort
gutra – the cloth of the headdress
hairaat – underwater sea mounds that were being developed as
    pearl banks
haluwsah – a children's game
hashu – a surface of fine stones
hawdaj – the elaborate saddle mounted on to camels for
    women's use
hdiba – a small low mound
hubara – the bustard, a favourite quarry for hunters
'irg or *sahib* – a small, narrow dune
jiri – poor pasturage area, but with water
jurn – horn-shaped hill
Kapucibasis – Ottoman honorific title, originally a palace
    gatekeeper
kaza – Ottoman district in eastern Arabia, including Qatar,
    Qatif, Hasa and Najd
khor – an inlet
khubz – bread
khutba – the Friday sermon at the midday prayer
majlis – a public council where individuals could raise grievances
mishaash – a temporary rock pool
mudir – a local Ottoman administrator
mujannah – wading on pearl banks in a tax-free end-of-season
    bid to get rich
musaqqam – a pearling industry financier
mutasarrifiyya – an Ottoman governorate
nagd – non-specific, general word for a dune
nahham – a singer who leads the shanty
naib – a deputy
naiim – low-lying grass suitable for grazing
najwaat – a pearl bank, usually around eight fathoms deep
nakhoda – a ship's captain
nakhsh – a prominent spur

Glossary

nigyan – the mini-dunes close to the shore that form a 'sea' of sand

niiga – a reddish dust that can settle after storms

qahwa della – a coffee pot with a curved spout

qasida – a form of poetry

Qayamaqam – an Ottoman title, meaning the head of a district

ramla – a small deposit of sand, in some parts of Qatar called a *bratha*

ras – a coastal cape

rawda – semi-permanent grazing area

razeef – a gathering of extended family, or tribal get-together

rigga – the smooth plains of the central plateau

rudaida – an end-of-season pearl hunt in a poor season

sabban – concentrated shell deposits, sometimes found inland

sayyal – the leeward, steep side of the dune

sbakha – low-lying salt pans

shi'b – stream course with a little vegetation

shimal – dust-bearing north-westerly wind

tawwash – a pearl merchant

tiwaar – flat-topped mesa

'ugla – a well in the southern desert

wa'ab – a geological depression, sometimes collecting water

wadi – a shallow valley

zakah – a religious tithe that was often imposed as a local tax

zubar – a medium-sized dune

zuli – the 'heads' on a Gulf-built ship

BIBLIOGRAPHY

Abdelaal, Ibrahim Ali, *British Policy towards Bahrain and Qatar 1871–1914*, Report, Lancaster: unpublished, 1988.

Abu Hakima, Ahmad Mustafa, *History of Eastern Arabia, 1750–1800: The Rise and Development of Bahrain and Kuwait*, Beirut: Khayats, 1965.

al-Dabagh, Mustafa Murad, *Qatar: Madiha Wa Hadiruha*, Beirut: Dar al-Taliha, 1961.

al-Fahim, Mohammed, *From Rags to Riches*, London: London Centre of Arab Studies, 1995.

al-Mansur, Abd al-Aziz, *Al-Tawattur al-Siyasi liQatar fi'l Fitra ma baina 1868–1916*, Kuwait: Dar Dhat al-Salasil, 1980.

al-Shaybani, Muhammad Sharif, *Imarat Qatar al-Arabiya bayn al-Maadi wa'l-Hadir*, Beirut: 1962.

al-Wazzan, Khalid and Abdullah al-Basimi, *al-Qayyim al-Diniya 'ind al-Shaikh Jassim bin Thani min khilal 'ilaqa bi-Najd wa 'ulamaha*, Riyadh: unpublished, 2008.

Anderson, Matthew, *The Eastern Question, 1774–1923: A Study in International Relations*, New York: St Martin's Press, 1966.

Anscombe, Frederick, *The Ottoman Gulf*, Blagoevgrad: Columbia, 1997.

JASSIM THE LEADER

Arkli, Engin, 'Economic policy and budgets in Ottoman
  Turkey, 1876–1909', *Middle Eastern Studies*, 3(28), Berkeley:
  University of California Press.
Bidwell, Robin, *Arabian Gulf Intelligence*, New York: Oleander
  Press, 1985, vol. XXIV and following.
Bidwell, Robin, *Arabian Personalities of the Early Twentieth Century*,
  New York: Oleander Press, 1986.
Bidwell, Robin, *The Affairs of Arabia, 1905–1906*, 2 vols, London:
  Frank Cass, 1971.
Bostan, Idris, 'The 1893 uprising in Qatar and Sheikh Al Thani's
  letter to Abdulhamid II', *Studies on Turkish–Arab Relations*, 2:
  81–8, 1987.
Busch, Briton, *Britain and the Persian Gulf, 1894–1899*, Berkeley:
  University of California Press, 1967.
Carter, Robert, 'The history and prehistory of pearling in the
  Persian Gulf', *Journal of Economic and Social History of the
  Orient*, 48(2), Leiden: Koninklijke Brill, 2005.
Cheesman, Capt. R. E., *In Unknown Arabia*, London: Macmillan,
  1926.
Davies, Charles, *The Blood Red Arab Flag*, Exeter: University of
  Exeter Press, 1997.
De Cardi, Beatrice, *Qatar Archaeological Report, Excavations*,
  Oxford: Oxford University Press, 1973.
Farah, Talal, *Protection and Politics in Bahrain, 1869–1915*, Beirut:
  American University of Beirut, 1985.
Gharayiba, Abd al-Karim, *Muqaddima Ta'rikh al-'Arab al-Hadith,
  1500–1918*, Damascus: Matba'a Jami'a Dimashq, 1960.
Graves, Philip, *The Life of Sir Percy Cox*, London: 1941.
Hamdoun, Abd ul-Aziz Ibrahim, *Qatar al-Haditha*, Doha:
  unpublished.
Hamzah, Fuad, *Qalb Jazirat al-Arab*, Cairo: al-Matba'a
  al-'Alamiya, 1933.

Bibliography

Harraz, Muhammad Rajab, *Al-Dawla al-'Uthmaniya wa Shibh Jazira al-'Arab, 1840–1909*, Cairo: al-Matba'a al-'Alamiya, 1970.

Historical Seminar, 'Jassim bin Muhammad bin Thani', Conference, Doha: Qatari Government, 16/17 December 2008.

Johnstone, T. and J. Wilkinson, 'Some geographical aspects of Qatar', *The Geographical Journal*, 126: 442–50, Oxford: Blackwell, 1966.

Kelly, John, *Eastern Arabian Frontiers*, London: Faber and Faber, 1964.

Kelly, John, *Britain and the Persian Gulf, 1795–1880*, Oxford: Clarendon Press, 1968.

Khatrash, Futuh and Abd al-Aziz al-Mansur, *Masadir Tar'ikh Qatar 1868–1916*, Kuwait: Dar Dhat al-Salasil, 1984.

Kursun, Zekeriya, *The Ottomans in Qatar*, Istanbul: Isis Press, 2002.

Lienhardt, Peter, 'The authority of shaikhs in the Gulf: an essay in nineteenth century history', *Arabian Studies*, II: 61–75, London: C. Hurst.

Lorimer, John, *Gazetteer of the Persian Gulf, Oman and Central Arabia*, vol. 1: *Historical*, Calcutta: Superintendent Government Printing, 1915.

Martin, William and Isabel, *Jassim*, Doha: Midas Press, 2008.

Miles, Colonel S. B., *The Countries and Tribes of the Persian Gulf*, London: Harrison, 1919.

Naqeeb, Hasan Khaldoun, *Society and State in the Gulf and Arabian Peninsula: A Different Perspective*, New York: Routledge, 1990.

Palgrave, William, *Personal Narrative of a Year's Journey through Central and Eastern Arabia, 1862–3*, London: Macmillan, 1883.

Pelly, Lewis, *Report on a Journey to Riyadh*, New York: Oleander Press, 1978.

Rahman, Habibur, *The Emergence of Qatar: The Turbulent Years 1627–1916*, London: Kegan Paul, 2005.

Ramadan, Mahmoud, *Qatar fi'l Khara'it al-Jaghraifiya wa'l-Tar'ikhiya*, Cairo: Markaz al-Hadara al-Arabiya, 2006.

Shahdad, Ibrahim, *Jassim al-Kabir wa siyasaatuhu fi fard al-shakhsiyat al-istiqlaliya li-Imarat Qatar*, Doha: Jami'at Qatar, 2008.

Sinan, Mahmoud, *Tar'ikh Qatar al-Aam*, Baghdad: 1966.

Tuson, Penelope, *The Records of the British Residency and Agencies in the Persian Gulf*, London: India Office Library and Records, 1979.

Wilkinson, John, *Arabia's Frontiers*, London: I. B. Tauris and Co., 1991.

Zahlan, Rosemarie Said, *The Creation of Qatar*, New York: Barnes and Noble Books, 1979.

INDEX

Brisk, HMS 138
Britain
  1835 agreement 13
  1868 agreement 93, 106, 139
  and Al bin Ali settlement in
    Zubara 141
  Anglo-Ottoman relations 108,
    109
  blockade of Qais 75
  control of Gulf's coastline 12
  defence of Bahrain 76, 78,
    82
  Governor-General's Council
    decree on tribute issue 85
  Indian Rebellion (1857) 77
  interest in internal affairs of
    Bahrain and Kuwait 168
  Jassim's attitude to 80, 81, 95
  makes Bahrain part of Trucial
    system (1861) 78
  Muhammad bin Thani favours
    an alliance 80
  and the Ottomans 83
  outraged at Jassim's change of
    allegiance 103–5
  and pearl trade 38, 39
  Perpetual Maritime Truce
    (1853) 13
  and Rahma 22–23
  relationship with Bahrain 12,
    73
  relationship with Muhammad
    bin Khalifa 84–85
  rule in India 9
  secret pact with Mubarak Al
    Sabah 147
  and slavery 33–34

  survey of the Gulf (1822–5)
    xviii, 49
  telegraphic cable laid between
    India and Iraq 99
  trade in Arabian Gulf 7
  treaty with Qatar (1916) 33
  tries to delay Suez project 98
  Trucial system 12
  unwillingness to commit
    troops in the Gulf 106
  worried about an Egyptian
    takeover of Bahrain 55
British Council 116
British Empire 31, 174
Brucks, Lieutenant (later
  Commodore) 49, 58, 59
Bubiyan island 162
Buhur bin Jubran 59
Bundar Jissah coaling station 162
Burchardt, Hermann xviii, 150
Burj al-Mah, Bida 73
Burton, Richard 61
Bushire, Iran 23, 93, 95, 119, 145

Caesar, Gaius 3
Cairo, French occupation of 97
Cartwright, Lieutenant
  Commander 145
Cheesman, Captain R.E. xviii
Chesney, Colonel 49
China, trade with 4, 6
Clive, HMS 56, 57
Clyde, HMS (gunboat) 81, 91
Coote, HMS 58
Correia, Antonio 7
Cox, Sir Percy 170–71, 181
Crimean War 108

Index

Index

Index

Perpetual Truce of Peace and
Friendship (1861) 78, 82, 90
Persepolis 2
Persia: relations with Qatar 2–3
Persia, Shah of 74
Philby, Harry St John ('Sheikh
Abdullah') 61
Phoenician merchants 2
Pigeon, HMS 144, 145
piracy 12, 13, 20, 21, 58, 59, 65,
71, 78, 111, 126, 131–32
Pirates of the Caribbean (film)
40
Plassey, HMS 144
Portugal
forced to withdraw 7, 8
violent domination of the
Gulf 7
Prideaux, Captain Francis Beville
16–17, 93, 160, 163, 171–72,
175–76, 178, 181
primogeniture 79
Psyche, HMS (survey vessel) xviii,
23, 49
Pyramus, HMS 181

Qais Island 56–57, 63, 66, 69, 72,
74, 75, 76
Qarmatians 5–6
Qasim, canonical judges 107
Qasimi navy 10, 11
Qasimi tribal confederacy 10–11
Qasimi-British War 10
Qasr al-Subaih 176
Qatar
achieves autonomy 179–82
Administrative Council 118

agreement of 1868 93, 106,
139, 185
and Bahraini dynastic disputes
62
British survey of (1822–5)
xviii, 49
camels in 4, 42–43, 112, 114
canonical judges 107
clan conflict 19
coastal settlement 167
destruction of villages xii
early references to xvi
economic conditions 172–73
fails to become part of Trucial
system 12
first roads and schools 41
gas reserves 186
geography xiii–xiv
horse breeding 4, 28
imports 43
Jassim's achievement as
founder of the modern state
xii, 181–82, 186
lack of agriculture 45
loss of strategic importance 3
the name xvii
Ottoman flags in 103, 104, 112,
141–42, 158, 177
Ottomans leave 15, 107
payment to Naim officially
removed (1880) 94
pearls help to provide for
Qatar's independence 31
politicised youth 50–57
problems of passing power in
166
relations with Persia 2–3

Index